RAISING CHILDREN TO LOVE GOD

RAISING CHILDREN TO LOVE GOD

BY TOMERRA DOMINIC

First Edition

Paperback ISBN: 979-8-9867009-0-8
eBook ISBN: 979-8-9867009-1-5

TABLE OF CONTENTS

INTRODUCING GOD

As I walked through the journey of writing this book, I asked God to help me share the things that He shared with me while parenting my children through each phase of their lives, from potty-training, all the way through young adulthood. My prayer is that in the same way that God has imparted to me His direction and wisdom, He will impart something to every parent reading this book, no matter the phase of parenting they are currently in. One of the most important things we can do for our children is to teach them about God. Teaching our children about God is just as important as ensuring that they have a good education and environment to grow up in. In fact, when we think about the leaders in the Bible, like Abraham and his children, we see that generation after generation, the knowledge of God was passed down. This was before modern-day education, replete with science and technology. Those things are certainly important in our ever-changing world, but our knowledge of God is critical to living a blessed life in this world.

Raising children who love God requires that they know God, have faith in God, and have a relationship with God. One critical aspect of imparting this information to our children is ensuring that we as parents know God for ourselves. The same trust in God and personal relationships with God that we want for our kids, we need first. Teaching something to someone else is hard to do when we have not genuinely experienced it for ourselves.

Accepting Christ as our Lord and Savior is the first step. The Bible says in Romans 10:9 that we should first call on the name of Jesus and confess that we are sinners and ask for His forgiveness. Then we should declare out loud, in faith, that we believe Jesus died on the cross and then rose again. The Bible says that when we have done that, we are saved and know that Jesus is our Lord and Savior. That's it. A very humble, sincere, and simple confession out of our mouths and a belief in our hearts that it is true are the beginning of our relationship with Jesus, the Son of God. When we have accepted Jesus as our Lord and Savior, we can be confident that we have all we need to raise children the way God intended us to raise them.

Teaching Kids about God

We will know when and how to teach them about who God is and why they should trust God. We can introduce our children to Him by explaining that God is a Father who created the world. We can point out that God created all things good. Teach them that God created the flowers and trees. Teach them that God made them, their brothers and sisters, their mom and dad. When they are very young, you don't have to worry about explaining how all of those things happen; the important thing is introducing Him as a God that is good, a God that loves them like a father, and a Father who sent His Son Jesus to the world to save us and that Jesus loves us too. When we are teaching them shapes and colors and numbers, it is just as important to introduce them to God the Father and Jesus the Son. As they get older, you can begin to explain in greater depth to them what God does for us and why we should love God, the Son, and the Holy Spirit.

The awesome thing about God, though, is that it doesn't matter how old you are when you acquire a relationship with Him. Knowing God is easy because all we have to do is ask to know Him. In Revelations 3:20 (NIV), God says, "Here I am! I stand at the door and knock. If anyone hears My voice and opens the door, I will come in to him and eat with that person, and they with Me."

My children were in elementary school when they made the decision to receive salvation. They could make that decision on their own, truly from their hearts, because they knew who Jesus was and that accepting Him as our Savior was a choice anyone could make. They asked to choose Jesus, and I said, "He is yours," and together we prayed the prayer in Romans 10:9.

Once we have accepted Christ as our Lord and Savior and our children have accepted Jesus as their Savior, we can rest in peace knowing that we will have eternal life together. John 6:40 (NIV) offers, "For my Father's will is that everyone who looks to the Son and believes in him shall have everlasting life; and I will raise them up at the last day." Everlasting life means there is a day when we will be in heaven forever with our children, God the Father, and Jesus the Son. Our children understand at a young age that having eternal life in the kingdom of God is a privilege and a wonderful place to be.

Once our children receive Jesus and eternal life, our prayers should then begin to focus on them having a relationship with God. It is important for them to have a personal relationship so they can live an abundant life filled with all the blessings God has for them on this earth. Our children need to have full access to God with a rich understanding of who He is. If your children receive Jesus at a young age, they don't have to understand every aspect of salvation and the sacrifice that Jesus made for us, but we certainly want them to at some point. We want our children to grow in God "like newborn babies, crave pure spiritual milk, so that by it [they] may grow up in [their] salvation now that [they] have tasted that the Lord is good" (1 Pet. 2:2–3 [NIV]).

Developing a relationship with God just requires us to talk to Him in prayer while standing in faith that He will answer us. Building faith in God requires us to believe in His promises, which are always good. The principles and promises found in His Word are simple—simple enough to teach our children. God's Word was always intended to be simple enough for a child to understand. Sometimes religion and tradition can make it appear complicated, but again, when we ask God to help us understand His principles to grow in our relationship with Him, He is faithful to show us.

Growing in our relationship with God enables us to grow in our faith as well. The Bible teaches that "without faith it is impossible to please God, because anyone who comes to him must believe that he exists and that he rewards those who earnestly seek him" (Heb. 11:6 [NIV]). So to have a genuine relationship with God, we must have faith.

Furthermore, the Bible defines faith as the "confidence in what we hope for and assurance about what we do not see" (Heb. 11:1 [NIV]). This means trusting God and His Word beyond our current circumstances. When our children understand this and continually grow in their faith, they become more confident in what they can do and their ability to overcome the trials they may face. Introducing and explaining a lifestyle of faith at a young age teaches children to be patient and steadfast. They also learn they can trust God for all things, even when their parents cannot be there to help.

I remember my son's first year of college was challenging for him. His school was a couple of hours away from home so he was not around his family, church, or friends. He struggled in his first-semester courses, and I could tell when I spoke with him there were things upsetting him. But he wrote me a letter that I will never forget. In it he told me about his grades, which were not very good, and some of the challenges he had faced. But most importantly, he said he knew he could do better because he could do all things through Christ, who strengthened him. I was proud to see the familiar scripture fueling his decision to work harder and proud that he was encouraging himself to walk by faith. During his second semester, his grades drastically improved, and he was a much happier young man. I was happier too. That mustard seed of faith was enough to show him that he could do better. After completing undergraduate and graduate school, he had achieved just shy of a 4.0 GPA.

Walking by faith and casting down doubt and worry can be challenging for all of us sometimes, even as parents. As believers, though, we can ask God to redeem us from doubt and strengthen our faith, patience, and endurance. Recognizing that we all have an opportunity to grow in faith, we should pray regularly that God increases our children's faith. Understanding that doubt is a strategy of Satan, we should continually ask God to build up our children in faith so they are armed to stand against the enemy. In Ephesians 6:16 (NIV) the Bible says to "take up the shield of faith, with which you can extinguish all the flaming arrows of the evil one."

The Importance of Spirit-Filled Kids

The Bible says we should train up our children in the way they should go and they will not depart from it. This wisdom constitutes great instruction for parenting because a parent can be assured that God's way will last forever. We want to know that when our children leave our homes to live on their own, they are equipped to walk a narrow path that Jesus will lead them on and that they will not stray too far away from. We want to be confident they have an independent godly relationship that is something beyond just a rule in our house that was to be followed, like cleaning their rooms or washing the dishes.

Godly children are ones who are filled with godly principles and values. When a child is taught godly principles, godly character and discipline become all the child knows. Everything new for the child has a foundation built in God's way and God's examples. Then the child's experiences and wisdom are developed with the instruction, direction, and promises that God's Word offers.

When our children are disobedient and sin, it is imperative that we speak with them about repentance and pray with them about their sins. The Bible teaches us to confess our sins, recognize that our actions were wrong, and ask God to forgive us. Teaching repentance to our children shows them that when we make mistakes, we can turn away from these mistakes and back to God and not live in condemnation and shame. They learn that God loves us despite our actions. Praying against the bondage of sin is critical because we want our children to learn from their sins and be free from the conviction of sin. The Bible says in Job 36:9–10 (AMP) that if we are bound in sin, He will reveal to us our deeds and transgressions and when we have sinned arrogantly, God opens our eyes to instruction and discipline. That passage of scripture goes on to teach about the fact that when we hear and obey, God promises a life of joy and prosperity but those who do not obey "perish by the sword and die without knowledge" (Job 36:12 [NIV]).

There are many places in the Bible that declare that sin leads to death but repentance leads to life. We want our children to understand that sin separates us from God and keeps us from living a full and abundant life. But the good news is that if we repent, we don't have to remain separated from God. God wants us to be reconciled with Him. If we as parents have taught this to our children, we can be secure in knowing they will not stray too far away from God and the life He wants us to live.

Wisdom acquired from scripture provides lessons that are hard to forget when they are ingrained in our hearts, minds, and souls. Children learn to love and trust God when parents draw their attention to the fact that God loves us and that His love is unfailing. A child's faith begins to grow when they see God's promises working in their lives. Teaching a child how to recognize God in their lives and how to appreciate and depend on God is one of the most important things we can do as parents.

As children grow older, they will attempt to align their actions with the principles they've learned and become familiar with. Most parents would agree that discipline and rules are important for a child or even an adult. However, rules should not be mistaken for godly principles. Rules are constructed on the basis of a principle. Rules can change over time or based on the situation. A child doesn't have the same rules at fifteen that they had when they were five. Rules for organizations or programs may only be applicable for one group. Divine principles are timeless and do not become outdated or pass away. The Bible says in Isaiah 40:8 (NIV) that "the grass withers, and the flowers fall but the word of our God endures forever."

For example, we might institute a "no fighting" rule for our children. We likely mandate this rule for several reasons. Certainly, we want our children to be safe and not hurt one another. However, simply telling our children not to fight does not necessarily teach them that fighting is a behavior that contradicts love and that it is hateful and rooted in evilness. It simply teaches them not to fight and break the rule. They may obey the rule to avoid punishment. When they are older, they may obey laws for the same reason—to avoid punishment. As we know, there are plenty of law-abiding citizens who do not live with godly principles. We want our children to obey a "no fighting" rule because the principle is that God says to love others. The hope is that when a child becomes angry enough to fight, they will choose not to because they want to please God.

The Bible says, "I have hidden your word in my heart that I might not sin against you" (Ps. 119:11 [NIV]). So helping our children see the difference between a rule and a godly principle is key. Rules that exist in the house should definitely align with God's principles, and we should take the time to show a child what the Bible says about them. When a child breaks a rule, we should also show them how their behavior contradicts the Word of God.

Kingdom Citizen Living

Unfortunately, we do not come into this world knowing the kingdom of God. We are all born into a world of sin in which we must be born again. We are either taught about God and

His goodness or we learn about it on our own. And sadly, some people do not accept the kingdom of God or the roles we play as kingdom citizens. It is our job as parents to teach the roles and responsibilities of kingdom citizen living. It is not enough to teach children that there is a God who lives in heaven and a devil who lives in hell. We have to teach them about the kind of God He is, His character and values, and how He expects us to live on this earth.

As Christians, we are given the high honor of living as citizens, ambassadors, and soldiers of the kingdom of God. These roles hold a significantly higher level of responsibility than those of any earthly kingdom and require our complete alignment and focus. We have the rights and responsibilities of living in the kingdom of God while living on earth. We have a dual citizenship, our physical kingdom with national borders and our kingdom citizenship established through Jesus Christ.

Teaching children how to live in the kingdom of God, especially at an early age, prepares them to live in an ever-changing world full of conflict and sin. It enables them to focus on a kingdom that transcends any earthly kingdom and prepares them to develop a perspective centered around a mission to share the gospel of Jesus Christ for all who desire eternal life. Living as kingdom citizens also prepares them for the glorious kingdom that awaits us in heaven.

Let me explain. Our role as citizen, ambassador, and soldier in the kingdom of God is a commandment given to every follower of Christ as a calling to fulfill the ministry of the gospel of Christ.

As kingdom citizens, we have been granted full access to the Spirit through Christ and hold the high honor of representing our Lord and Savior, Jesus Christ. Our rights include a God who is all-knowing, all-seeing, and all-sufficient who has sent us a righteous and redeeming and present Lord who grants us peace, provision, and healing. The scripture says that "For through him we both have access by one Spirit to the Father. So, then you are no longer strangers and aliens, but you are fellow citizens with the saints and members of the household of God, built on the foundation of the apostles and prophets, Christ Jesus himself being the cornerstone" (Eph. 2:18–19 [NKJV]).

Our responsibilities include our performance in our roles as ambassadors and soldiers because these roles are key to how we project and represent our King to the world. According to John 10:10 (NIV), when children understand what citizenship means, they can live a full life with every privilege citizens are given. As they grow physically and encounter new things, they can hold themselves account-able but are also privileged as they grow in wisdom through the study of God's Word.

An ambassador is defined as a diplomatic representative of one country or kingdom sent as a messenger to another country or kingdom. As kingdom citizens, we must be foreign ambassadors to the secular world. Ephesians 6:19–20 (NIV) says, "Pray also for me, that whenever I speak, words may be given me so that I will fearlessly make known the mystery of the gospel, for which I am an ambassador in chains. Pray that I may declare it fearlessly, as I should." Our message can be delivered through our own personal testimony, demonstrated by our Christlike behavior, or exercised in our God-given purpose or mission. A kindergartener can be an effective ambassador of Christ if they are taught to be kind and loving to others, submissive and cooperative with authority. Encouraging participation in the kingdom with the heart and mind demonstrated by Jesus cultivates our children into faithful ambassadors regardless of their age.

As soldiers, we are employed to serve in the army of the kingdom. The Word says in 2 Timothy 2:1–4 (ESV), "You then, my child, be strengthened by the grace that is in Christ Jesus, and what you have heard from me in the presence of many witnesses entrust to faithful men, who will be able to teach others also. Share in suffering as a good soldier of Christ Jesus. No soldier gets entangled in civilian pursuits, since his aim is to please the one who enlisted him." Notice the instruction to avoid becoming "entangled in civilian pursuits." This means we should not prepare our children to battle or align with social groups or ideologies that desire to influence government but instead "put on the full *armor of God*, so that [we] can take [our] stand against the devil's schemes" (Eph. 6:11 [NIV]).

Just knowing that there is a God does not help anyone to develop a relationship with Him or learn how He thinks and acts. Because God lives in a spiritual world that we cannot see, we won't know about Him unless we hear about Him through the Spirit or by a messenger He has sent. In contrast, the world is a place that we do see. Therefore, our children will grow in a world surrounded by things that do not represent or resemble God. It might be easy for them to mimic and believe what they see, especially if they are not introduced to and reminded about anything different.

As the Spirit leads us, we should explain how earthly and fleshly things differ from a Spirit-filled life where our eyes and thoughts are focused on heaven. While our children grow and change physically, Paul tells us in 2 Corinthians 4:16–17(NIV) that we should not focus on the things seen but rather on the unseen: "Therefore, we do not lose heart. Though outwardly we are wasting away, yet inwardly we are being renewed day by day. For our light and momentary troubles are achieving for us an eternal glory that far outweighs them all." Furthermore, Colossians 3:1–4 (NIV) advises, "Since, then, you have been raised with Christ, set your hearts on things above, where Christ is, seated at the right hand of God. Set your minds on things above, not on earthly things. For you died, and your life is now hidden with Christ in God. When Christ, who is your life, appears, then you also will appear with him in glory."

The ability, by the power of the Holy Spirit, to focus on the heavens above and unseen things broadens and reshapes how we see all aspects of the world (people, politics, technology, science, economy, history, art, etc.). This focus builds a foundation of successful kingdom citizen living that encourages our children to view everything through the lens of biblical scripture.

Knowing and being able to recognize both kingdoms is important because they will shape our values, how we think, and what we believe. Our values, thoughts, and beliefs are what determine our decisions, attitudes, and actions.

As our children grow, all sorts of ideas, opinions, resources, philosophies, traditions, and histories will compete with the Bible to establish a belief system in our children's hearts and minds. However, the Bible instructs us not to conform to the world's superficial values and customs but to renew our minds in the Word of God (Rom. 12:2 [NIV]). It is important that we embrace that instruction for ourselves and our children as we grow and spiritually mature. This type of restoration and development happens when the mind is continually focusing on the godly values, attitudes, and behavior found in the Word of God. As new things of the world are introduced to our children, again, we must address how they differ from what the Bible says. When we focus on what God's Word says and not what the world says, God will prove to us that His divine principles are right. He will continually show us that if we trust in Him and obey His Word, He will take care of us and direct us in the way that we should go.

Establishing the Word of God as the source of truth in our lives is key to teaching our children about God and His kingdom. We have to enforce that there can be no other source of truth outside the Bible. As we consistently discuss the differences between God and the world with our children, they will begin to assess ideas and opinions according to what the Bible says on their own. The Bible tells us that what is ingrained in the heart is what will come out of us through our choices and decisions. When we truly believe something, that is what we walk in. What we believe is inherent to how we act. Therefore we want our children to independently develop their own belief systems founded in the Word of God. And ultimately, we want them to be wise enough to know the Word of God is true.

WHAT DO GODLY CHILDREN LOOK LIKE?

So what do godly kids look like? What are their characteristics, and how do they stand out among others? How do they become lights in a world of darkness?

Kids that love the Lord are not perfect kids who never disobey or misbehave. They certainly do their fair share of that! Just as all of us have discipline and obedience challenges, so will they. What we are looking for is to have their characteristics resemble the character of Jesus, just as ours should.

These kids are respectful, helpful, inquisitive, supportive, and giving. They are good leaders, good students, and good workers. They're independent, resourceful, courageous, unafraid to stand out and set high standards for themselves. They are also thankful, kind, loving, and encouraging to others.

These characteristics resemble what the Bible calls the Fruits of the Spirit. The Bible is referring here to the Holy Spirit and says that those who belong to Christ will live by the Holy Spirit and will be led by the Holy Spirit to generate fruit or characteristics of the Holy Spirit. The characteristics of the Spirit are love, joy, peace, patience, kindness, goodness, faithfulness, gentleness, and self-control. When you as the parent require these standards for their behavior, you will see those characteristics develop in your child.

Others will also see those characteristics in your children because they will stand out, even if those people are not familiar with the Fruits of the Spirit or do not know Jesus for themselves. Requiring standards and certain behavior from your children consistently throughout their development will instill in them that this is good and right and that behavior contrary to these standards is ungodly. Requiring your children to be respectful, helpful, giving, thankful, and loving at home won't seem so foreign to them when you require it outside of the home.

Encouraging your children in their goals with scripture allows them to grow in their faith. As encouragers themselves, children will learn how to be compassionate toward others while also developing very strong leadership skills at a very young age.

Motivated Learners

We also want our children to be inquisitive, detail-oriented, and resourceful. Motivate them to ask questions, and take the time to explain things with patience. Show them how to look for things with an expectation to learn and desire to grow in their knowledge and understanding. They will become strong, independent students and workers. These leadership skills will be apparent throughout their developmental years and onward into young adulthood.

For some children, the desire to learn just comes naturally. They seem to just come out of the womb asking questions. They follow their parents around asking "why?" about everything! That is OK because inquisitive children also become creators, teachers, developers, and problem-solvers.

Other children may not appear to be inquisitive because they like to learn by observing. They observe and analyze and consider both sides of everything. That is OK too because this still shows a natural desire to understand. Regardless of how our children embrace learning, our job is to foster their learning style and pray that the motivation to learn is embedded deep in their hearts. We pray not only for their desire to learn but also for our patience to teach. That means we answer questions with enthusiasm and not frustration or annoyance, even when we are tired or busy. We take the time to ask children questions when we are talking to them or explaining things rather than just assuming they understand what we have said. We inquire about what they are thinking and encourage them to share all of their ideas.

Learning also requires disciplining our children to listen. Staying engaged and fostering good listening skills can be more challenging for some than others. When my son was a preschooler, sitting still in the circle for story time was a challenging task for him. Teachers would consistently tell me what a joy he was to have in their class but that sitting still was not his strongest skill. So, during our study time at home, we played a familiar game called "crisscross, applesauce" which requires the participant to cross one leg over the other to practice sitting still and improve their discipline of listening.

As my son got older, pediatricians and teachers repeatedly presented the possibility that he could have attention deficit hyperactivity disorder (ADHD). The recommendations were to treat the disorder with medicine and have my son meet with child psychologists. When I took the time to read about ADHD and the signs and symptoms (inattention, impulsivity, and hyperactivity) associated with it, I came to view them not as a disorder in my son but rather as a lack of self-control. This was evidence that his listening skills were challenges we could address but the situation certainly did not warrant medicine and therapy. I believe that had I accepted the diagnosis and proposed treatment, I would have risked allowing strongholds to develop in his life.

A spiritual stronghold is a faulty thinking pattern based on lies and deception. One of the primary weapons of the devil is invoking doubt and deception, which are necessary for a stronghold to take root and become something we accept as truth. In actuality, strongholds prevent us from receiving God's best for us. For my son, I was concerned that using medicine to control his behavior would create a physical dependence and belief that he could not change without the drugs. I also believed that no one knew him better than the Lord and I, so having him meet with psychologists to improve his focus did not seem like the best option for us either. Praying for his behavior and the guidance I needed on how to instill self-control seemed to be the best approach for us. God showed Himself faithful. My son's attentiveness and his desire to learn grew stronger and stronger the older he got. As an adult, he chose to pursue a career that requires extreme focus and a desire to read and analyze information daily. I am so grateful we trusted God and not medicine.

In the Book of Proverbs, the Word of God reminds us over and over again of the importance of knowledge and advises us to "Hold on to instruction, do not let it go; guard it well, for it is your life" (Prov. 4:13 [NIV]). So in commitment to obeying the Word of God, we can ask that He prepare our minds with clear pathways for learning and organize our minds in a way that makes learning enjoyable and not burdensome.

We should pray not only for our children's ability and motivation to listen and learn but also for the teachers they encounter. The responsibility of teaching children day after day is not an easy assignment, and I have so much respect and appreciation for all those who do it well. Asking God to place teachers in our children's lives that encourage and foster their strengths and gifts is very important. We want teachers, mentors, and other influential adults involved in their lives to have the strength and desire to listen and motivate.

We must also seek God on our children's behalf that they are able to hear the voice of the Lord. As they grow in their relationship with God, their ear to hear the Holy Spirit and discern the wisdom of God is what will enable them to seek God and understand His spiritual guidance. When you hear the Word of God without an understanding of it, you cannot apply the wisdom in your own life. When choices arise and we are not there to lead and guide, we need our children to understand the guidance of the Holy Spirit. We want the direction of the Holy Spirit to be clear to them in those times of decision-making. Clear direction comes from an understanding of the Word and a relationship with God that enables them to hear when God is speaking to them. Good learning experiences in school complement learning experiences in life, and vice versa. The Word of God says, "the wise will hear and increase their learning, and the person of understanding will acquire wise counsel and the skill" (Prov. 1:5 [AMP]). No matter what circumstances, environments, or disabilities we face, we can be assured that if we seek the wisdom of God, we can attain all the knowledge and wisdom we need. Our reverence and fear of the Lord give us access to the knowledge and wisdom of God.

God-Fearing

The fear of the Lord is critical in our work with God. When we seek His wisdom, it is important that we also develop a deep desire to apply the Word in our lives. Fearing the Lord means respecting Him and His authority in our life. Fearing the Lord also means wanting to be pleasing only to Him, above our own flesh and pride. "To fear the Lord is to hate evil; I hate pride and arrogance, evil behavior and perverse speech" (Prov. 8:13 [NIV]), says the Lord. It also means a desire to serve Him with a gratefulness that He lives in us and that the Holy Spirit can use us for God's purpose.

So how do we teach our children to have that kind of reverence for God and to want to obey and seek Him with all their hearts? When we read the Word of God to them and show them in the scriptures the instructional part of God's Word, it enables them to see that God wants us to do something. God doesn't just expect us to figure it out on our own. And although He wants us to obey His instruction, it is not hard to do. We show our children that obedience to God always yields blessings in our lives so they understand fearing God is not a bad thing. It is a healthy form of worship that demonstrates how much we love Him. Fearing God means that we have so much respect for Him because He loves us so much. We want to serve Him out of a thankfulness for who He is in our lives. Disciplining our children to recognize when their own actions do not align with God's instruction teaches them to have a sincere heart to obey Him. When we pray for them, we ask God to allow them to see the joy and peace in serving and seeking Him.

God-Seeking

Children who have a relationship with Christ and believe they are equipped by the power of Christ can develop a "Yes, Lord, I will go" mindset. This mindset says, "Use me, Lord, for your will and your work." As members in the body of Christ, we all have work to do. To be clear, it is not a job we all have to do; it is *work*. There is a difference. The main purpose of doing a job is to earn money. Any activity you do in exchange for monetary payment is a "job." Work, however, can be done either to earn money or to perform a general task. Work also has a broader, general objective to achieve a goal whereas a job is specific to acquiring a resource. For example, a teacher receives pay in their job to teach children, while the same person might work as a volunteer to teach. The task is the same, but unlike a job, work is not done with the expectation of pay. Work in the body of Christ is what God has already equipped us to do for His purpose, for His goals, and with no personal expectation of our own except to serve Him.

The Bible encourages us to go and teach the message of the gospel to all. Some of the greatest evangelists in the Bible were not trained to evangelize. In fact, many of them were skilled in other areas that enabled them to perform other jobs. The Bible shows us that James and John, two of Jesus's closest disciples, were skilled fishermen when they were asked to be followers of Christ. Most of the New Testament is written by Paul, who originally held a job as a tax collector. The work they did for Christ was based on a willing heart and desire to serve Christ. Sharing the gospel of Christ required the disciples to (1) stand up, (2) go out, and (3) speak about the message they were receptive to doing. All of us are already prepared and equipped for this same work in one form or another.

We need our children—and future generations—to be willing to stand up and be used as vessels of God. As parents, we should do all we can to help them develop skills and talents and identify their gifts, but the focus should not be on a job. The focus should be on developing work that God has intended for us all to do. That's where we find our purpose and passion.

Encouraging our children to work in ministry is one way of encouraging them in work. It shows them that work can help others and be fun and is inspired by God—that all they must do to excel in it is to say, "Yes, Lord." As they grow, their work in ministry will change and grow. Ensuring that children are interested in and committed to serving in the body of Christ stems from a parent's own commitment to serving. If children see their parents serving and actively participating in helping others, they will naturally want to follow that example. Even when they are young, involving them in whatever way you can is good. In fact, having them participate in church ministries or community service while they are young is *extremely* important. Finding ways to do so should not be hard either.

You can invite them to help you with simple tasks in your service to others. If you bake or donate food to others who are ill or disadvantaged, allow them to help you with preparing the food and explain what you are doing. As they get older, if you serve in the music ministry at your church, encourage them to join you in that ministry or attend rehearsals or invite them to help you set up equipment. If you are attending a church that regularly sponsors programs and activities in the community, it will likely seek volunteers to help. Sign up, and take your children when possible. Explain the purpose of the program and what you will be doing to help. Depending on their age, there may be all kinds of small things they can do to assist.

If your church does not sponsor a lot of community-based or other ministry opportunities within the church, perhaps you can speak with the pastor about leading some. I've helped lead youth "shut-ins" where children of all ages were invited to stay overnight at the church participating in activities such as Bible teachings, games, question and answer sessions, group discussions, and singing praise and worship music. If you have a passion for music and drama, you can volunteer to direct a youth choir or direct Christian-based skits and plays. There are lots of resources online offering free scripts with a Christian message.

These activities are very inexpensive to sponsor and can be easy to implement. In addition, developing a heart to give to others does not always have to involve a direct connection with your church. Signing up with nonprofit organizations that support the needs of others is also a great way to serve. For example, if you are particularly passionate about medical research for a particular disease, disadvantaged youth, abused women or children, and so on, you can likely find an organization online that you can serve. My job offers annual community service days and opportunities to participate in clothing and food drives.

Your children's school may also offer activities that are not ministry-based. Allow your children to attend and be involved in these activities. Attending these types of events builds confidence within children to speak to others about Christ. I am a big advocate of nonprofit organizations designed for youth. The Girl Scout and Boy Scout organizations continue to be two of the best nonprofits for providing developed, age-appropriate volunteer activities for children. Both of my children participated in these programs. It is easy to find a group in your area by searching for their websites.

I also believe that helping children to become God-seekers means encouraging them to participate in church services. In church my children were required to stand up and sing along in the praise and worship songs with everyone else. They were not allowed to do other things during prayer time. Praying in church and at home meant being still and quiet, listening and respecting that this was a special time.

Eventually, after we talked about God and referenced and applied scripture in their lives throughout the week, Sunday-morning worship service began to mean something to them. They understood they were worshipping a real God they had talked about and experienced all week long in their lives. Whether they chose to share their feelings about the service with me or not, as they got older, I could see the sincerity in their worship toward God. There was genuine reverence, and giving thanks, honor, and glory to God was something sacred and enjoyable to them. They wanted more from their own personal relationship with God.

Fortunately, we also attended a church that had children's services. Once the praise and worship service was complete, the children were invited to leave the main sanctuary to attend the youth services in another part of the church. I was grateful for "Children's Church." My children were learning about God in a way that would make sense to them, which was not something I experienced in the church I grew up in. The message was built around activities and content appropriate to their age and kept them engaged. Whether our churches have services dedicated for the youth or not, we should still look for Christian-based activities outside the church for our children to participate in. This provides an opportunity for them to fellowship with other believers in their own age range.

Leaders in the Body of Christ

As you point out opportunities for them to lead others, teach them how a good leader can positively affect someone else. The Bible says that when we plant seeds in good ground, they will grow and multiply.

I can remember when both of my children wanted to run for the office of student representative in middle school. They were both afraid they would not be elected and decided not to run. I encouraged them to think about what a good representative would do and asked them whether they could do it.

My daughter enjoyed art and crafting, and so she made ribbons that students could wear to encourage others to vote for her. My son made a poster with characteristics of good leadership skills and included a cute picture of himself demonstrating each of those skills. They were both elected, but they had to step out in faith and be confident enough to represent themselves as leaders first. They had to first believe that they could do it. I also wanted them to know they were prepared to do it through the power of Jesus Christ.

In Philippians 4:13 (NKJV), Paul says to the Philippian church, "I can do all things through Christ who strengthens me." This was a very popular scripture in our home. I am not exaggerating when I say we probably proclaimed it at least once a week! I will probably reference it several more times in this book. I also taped that scripture, along with a few other scriptures, to the bathroom mirror where my children brushed their teeth. They were so frequently reminded of that scripture because we took "all things" quite literally. Where we were weak, we could depend on accomplishing the thing through Christ's strength. As a result, the words "I can't do it" were not really ever accepted. To this day it is a scripture we use to proclaim power to accomplish things through Jesus.

As the kids got older, participating in youth activities at the church and in the community became a matter of their desire instead of my invitation or suggestion. They volunteered for roles with accountability, and they encouraged others to do the same. They attended youth Bible studies with peers who were also eager to study the Word of God. They were not afraid to invite others to join them. When my son began his internship the summer after he graduated from college, he decided to organize a lunchtime Bible study at the company where he was working. After my daughter completed her own domestic and international work as a Christian missionary, she decided to mentor high school and college students in preparation and discipleship for their own mission trips.

Working in the body of Christ will also teach children that while a successful life is important, it is also important to have a significant life, a life where they say yes to a God-given purpose geared toward helping others rather than just pursuing a job for money.

As the kids were working to complete college and making decisions about a career, I noticed they were not drawn to a career choice based on a salary range. I never directed them to do this, but they were just always interested in careers that would enable them to help or serve others. In fact, I probably did the opposite and encouraged them to pursue high-paying careers. It is what I was taught as a child and all I knew to do. "Go to college, get a good job, and earn some good money" was what I heard all my life and what I focused on in my own life. I frequently discussed financial management and the importance of good stewardship while the kids were growing up in my home because I did not want them to struggle financially once they were on their own, like I did. While good stewardship is important, seeking money above God's work is not what God has called us to do.

When my son graduated from college, he worked in corporate America for a while and then went on to serve in the United States Army. While he was working for a very successful corporation and earning a very good salary, he didn't seem to be satisfied. He always had the desire to "defend and protect." He was the only male in the house, and even when he was a child, he wanted to take care of his sister and me. I also remember how he used to say he wanted to be a firefighter to save other people. His spiritual gifts in leadership and administration, teaching, exhortation, knowledge, and wisdom worked nicely with his role in the army, and he was able to succeed and advance very quickly.

My daughter's role as a surgical neurophysiologist was also very promising. In this position, she monitored patients' nerve activity during surgery and advised neurosurgeons on how to respond while they performed surgeries. Although she enjoyed helping during these important procedures, she just did not feel she was fulfilling her purpose. This job did not allow her to fully operate in her spiritual gifts of evangelism, discernment, healing, prophecy, teaching, encouragement, leadership, and administration. She was OK with walking away from a well-paying position in order to walk into a purpose-driven one. She left the job to begin working with a nonprofit Christian organization that sponsored international mission trips around the world. When she returned home, she began working in a shelter for abused women and children, leading devotional worship services and programs focused on the Word of God.

The kids were interested in adding value to the work and not just checking off the task. Becoming a person of value is what God wants us to do. Value or significance is all about providing meaning or quality to something or someone, not just accomplishing a task. Accomplishing a task does not always entail a significant outcome. A millionaire can declare themselves successful at the goal of becoming rich. By today's standards, this sort of success is measurable by how much money one has. But being rich does not necessarily mean you've helped someone else. For a person to declare themselves significant is more of a challenge. It is harder to independently measure. In Mark 10:17-22 (NIV), a wealthy man approaches Jesus and tells him that he has kept all the Lord's commandments since he was a boy and he asks Jesus what he must do to inherit eternal life. Jesus replies "One thing you lack, go, sell everything you have and give to the poor, and you will have treasure in heaven. Then come, follow me." The Bible says the man walks away very sad because he was not willing to sell his riches.

Significance generally requires another person to attest to whether something was important or valuable to them. While we must teach our children to thoroughly complete their tasks, we must also ask them to look for ways to accomplish those tasks with a desire to offer meaning and value to someone else. Then we must pray that others will follow in the same manner. This is how the body of Christ grows.

My daughter continues to evangelize and serve in her international missionary work. She believes that in America we are so privileged to not only have the exposure to Christ but also the freedom to choose Jesus Christ as our Lord and Savior. While preparing for an eleven-month international mission trip, she stated, "How can someone have a relationship with the Lord if they've never heard His name? I cannot imagine what my life would be like without God's presence and a relationship with Him. I want to share the love and hope of Jesus Christ!" She has ministered in countries in South America, Asia, Africa, Europe, and the Middle East with that same passion for introducing Jesus to those who do not know Him.

My son has also developed a nonprofit organization focused on helping young adults tear down barriers, such as economic, physical, and emotional disadvantages, that could hinder them from growing. Programs and services are intended to be Christ-centered and founded on the belief that Jesus Christ is our Lord and Savior and that God's calling for His children is to serve others. The programs and initiatives include financial aid, leadership and life skills, spiritual advisement, and educational assistance to youth, their families, and others in need. The core values of the organization are to (1) give, (2) hope, (3) inspire, (4) believe, (5) grow, and (6) lead.

As young adults, both of my children are continuing to spiritually grow and advance in the Word of God. They both walk in their spiritual gifts to serve and lead. When they hear or experience something good and new, they naturally want to share it with someone else. "Go ye therefore and teach all nations" was another familiar scripture in our home.

PURPOSEFUL PARENTING

As Christians, we recognize that God has designed us with a purpose. He tells us in Jeremiah 29:11 that he knows the plans he has for us. I viewed parenting as a purposeful plan that God created me to execute. However, recognizing that incredible responsibility, I grew fearful that I would fail or mess up. I saw the purpose as divine and my children as gifts, and I wanted to do everything right. I wondered; How do I do that?

I even remember after the kids went off to college, I found myself in a terrible state of depression. I was working in a job where I was not happy. I was bored, stressed, and felt like this could not be God's purpose for me. For so many years, I had been focused on raising the children. Many of my goals, plans, and accomplishments seemed focused on the kids. I felt raising godly children and doing my part as a mother had to do with God ultimately doing His part in their lives. I was so afraid that I would mess up and prevent them from experiencing all that God had prepared for them. When they left for school, the house was empty. My life slowed down. My job of being a taxi-cab driver for all of their activities was over. My trips were only to the office, grocery store, and back home. That was it.

During that depression, though, I began to press in very hard in my prayer time because I just could not accept that my God-given purpose was behind me. Eventually, I realized that my purpose was ongoing. When I began to seek Him about my purpose, He showed me that writing this book could be a part of my purpose to help others and the only thing preventing me from walking in it was the choice not to do it. Writing the book wasn't dependent on my job and tasks associated with parenting or whether anyone was in the house or not. The book was about my willingness to say, "Yes, Lord, I will do it" and about the significance it could provide to someone else.

In my pursuit of purpose and how He could use me, I also realized the years of worrying that I would mess up the kids' purpose were not necessary. I learned that I cannot mess up anything that God has given; I can only not use it. My part in the kids' purpose was to teach them who God is and that God has given them each a purpose to use in the body of Christ, to show them that seeking a purpose means seeking Him.

Parenting in Pain

The feelings of rejection I felt from my own childhood and marriage constantly reinforced my fears of failing as a parent. Having been raised by my grandparents and an aunt and uncle, I always felt I had done something wrong or there was some reason my parents were not around or did not want to be an active part of my life.

The kids were very young when their father and I separated and eventually divorced. How was I going to make my children feel loved when I didn't feel loved?

I viewed my failed marriage as one aspect of failing as a parent. I wanted my children to have a father in the home. It hurt to think about the possibility of my kids growing up believing they were not loved. I wanted to make sure I loved them enough that I did not impart to them the feelings of rejection and hurt I felt from my own life. As much as I loved them, I was constantly wondering if my love was going to be enough.

I remember crying out to the Lord one day and saying, "Father, I have no idea how to raise these kids." I asked the Lord to show me how to make sure my kids knew they were loved by me and God the Father. I asked God to be their Heavenly Father and in the absence of their earthly father, to provide them with everything they needed. God was so faithful to hear my prayer!

Living Free of Unforgiveness

The first thing He showed me was that unforgiveness is just a tool of the enemy that keeps us all bound in pain. I realized that part of my own pain was fueled by still being in a place of unforgiveness toward my parents and the children's father. I still blamed them for every failure and mistrial in my own life. I viewed growing up without my parents as the reason my marriage failed. As much as I wanted to prevent this kind of pain in my children's lives, I eventually realized that parenting in unforgiveness was not healthy for any of us.

I began to see I had to lay down the burden of rejection and choose to focus on the joy of knowing God's love for me was unconditional and everlasting. I saw that despite all of my mistakes, God had and always would love me. I began to see that a lot of different factors had led to the outcomes of all my past relationships, including the broken ones. These things helped me to see God as the all-forgiving God that He is. It became clear that if God forgave me for all of my mistakes, He must really love me. Forgiveness was a huge step for me being able to begin moving on with my life. My goal had always been for the children to feel loved and not to inherit feelings of resentment toward others. Therefore, as hard as it was to see how uninvolved the children's father was in their lives, I refused to talk negatively about him. I would not harp on times when he did not respond or focus on his unkept promises. I focused on sharing my love with them and teaching them about God's love for them.

God was even faithful enough to allow me to build a relationship with my mother. Once I was able to open a door of forgiveness in my heart, I could see she wanted to be a part of my life and my children's lives. I'm so grateful that I did not limit that relationship based on things that happened in the past. They *love* their grandmother, and she is blessed with joy in her heart at the sound of their names!

Enjoying Freedom from Fear

God also helped me to understand that it was impossible for me to do everything right. I had to learn to accept that making mistakes as a parent did not mean that I loved my children any less. It also did not mean that I had ruined their lives or somehow destroyed God's plan for their lives. Those fears sound pretty extreme, but I can honestly say, that's how I felt.

Understanding that I was not God, the perfect parent, freed me from a lot of anxiety. It was another burden I learned to lay down. I could see that where I was lacking, His grace would truly be sufficient. His strength and power would be made perfect in my weakness (2 Cor. 12:9 [NIV]). As a single parent, I had to remind myself of that scripture often. I prayed to God that He would teach me to be the parent he desired me to be and allow the Holy Spirit to show me when I made a mistake. I asked God to allow me to hear the Holy Spirit and be humble enough to receive the guidance, repent, and move on.

When I cried out to God to help me as a parent, I was trusting that He was a true Father to us and the best parent there is. I believed that He knew better than I and that His wisdom was needed. I was hoping He would answer my prayers and show me how to love them and that He would love us perfectly. He did just that with His unconditional love.

If we as parents open our hearts to God the Father, all we have to do is obey His Word. All His instruction is in His

Word. That is a *choice* and not a *deficiency* for any parent. The one thing we must do is understand that our children are gifts to us from God. It is a privilege that He gave them to us. All He wants us to do is give them back to Him. We do that by introducing them to God and teaching them about who He is.

That means more than just church on Sunday and hanging a cross in your house. It means knowing Him yourself and teaching your children how to walk like Jesus walked. It is not hard, and if you have an obedient heart, God will not let you fail. He says, "Do not be anxious about anything, but in every situation, by prayer and petition, with thanksgiving, present your requests to God" (Phil. 4:6 [NIV]).

Receiving a Sound Mind

The Word of God tells us that "God has not given us the spirit of fear; but of power, and of love, and of a sound mind" (2 Tim. 1:7 [KJV]). I receive this scripture to mean that God wants me to be confident in my decisions and choices, walk in joy and peace, and have a focused mind. God does not want me to be insecure, in turmoil, and confused. But a reasonable question would be, How do we know we are functioning in what God has intended for us? How do we know we are making decisions with a spirit of power and love and operating with a sound mind as the leaders of our households? How do we overcome feelings of insecurity, turmoil, and confusion?

Paul gives direction in Romans 12:2 that provides answers to these questions, if we choose to obey. The Amplified Version of the Bible says, "And do not be conformed to this world (any longer with its superficial values and customs), but be transformed and progressively changed [as you mature spiritually] by the renewing of your mind (focusing on godly values and ethical attitudes), so that you may prove (for yourselves) what the will of God is, that which is good and acceptable and perfect (in His plan and purpose for you)."

When we renew our minds in the values and attitudes of the Lord, which can be found in scripture, we choose to accept holy living over worldly customs, tradition, and unholy values. Renewing your mind means keeping the Word of God active and fresh in your mind. It's also our job to keep the Word of God fresh in our children's minds.

I forwarded the "Verse of the Day" found on Bible.com to my children every morning while they were away at college. I wanted to keep their minds renewed with scripture even though they were away from home and church. It is amazing how reading one scripture per day from your cell phone can keep you focused with a mind centered around God. I even found that somehow that verse of the day spoke directly to me about the current situation in my life or in my children's lives. The Word of God never changes, nor does it ever conflict with itself. However, it will supply new meaning to your life whenever it is needed.

When we are keeping our minds focused on God and our choices and decisions align with His values, we can be confident we are operating in a spirit of power and love. He is the all-powerful God, ruler of all things, the alpha and omega, the beginning and the end. So when we abide in the Word and obey it, we can trust our decisions and choices are made with God's power, which we inherit through our relationship with Jesus Christ.

The same is true for love. Christ is our example of walking in love. One of the most powerful ways you can ensure that you and your children are incorporating and growing in a spirit of love is to ask yourself, "What would Jesus do if he were making the choice I need to make?" The Bible says Jesus was fully man and fully God. This tells me that Jesus experienced everything we as men, women, and children experience today, only he handled those situations perfectly, as God. We won't always perform perfectly, but we can follow Jesus's example.

We can also be assured that we are able to walk in a sound mind without doubt and confusion. Scripture, Old Testament and New, does not contradict itself or lead us down rabbit holes. The scriptures, and especially God's commands, are direct and to the point. Some of my favorite scriptures are God's promises. They are very simplistic and often come in the form of "if/then" instruction. God tells us that *if* we do something, *then* this will happen. I have never found those promises to fail me or my children.

Parenting with Integrity

I knew that parenting with purpose meant parenting with integrity, something I could give God the glory for. My motivation was that one day I would have the honor of hearing God tell me, "Well done, my good and faithful servant" for the work I have done as a parent and in the body of Christ.

The idea of God being pleased with the way I raised my children was very important to me. It meant that my children had been given back to Him as useable vessels on earth and in the kingdom of God with an understanding of their own purpose-filled lives.

Raising children with godly integrity means ensuring your choices and decisions regarding your family honor God, and demonstrate God is the ruler and ultimate decision-maker in your home. The activities you engage in, the entertainment and behavior you allow to be a part of your home and family, must honor God. If God cannot look down at the decision and be pleased with it, then it is not something a parent should feel comfortable with for themselves or their children.

Parenting with integrity also means that you are wholly invested in the things God asks of us. You are not divided on what you believe because one concept is more comfortable or more socially acceptable. In today's culture it's so easy to be influenced by what the government, media, or religion tells us is right or OK to accept. Even when the intent is to follow God, we must examine everything in the light of how God views it. God has an answer for everything in His Word. It's our job to choose His Word.

Teaching Children the Word of God

God's Word always comes with principles, promises, and instructions. An important aspect of teaching children the Word of God is having them memorize key scripture. I encouraged the kids to memorize scripture for a few reasons: I wanted them to be able to encourage themselves with God's Word when I was not around, and in those situations, I wanted them to confidently stand in that Word and not have to struggle to remember what God's Word says. It was also important so they could begin to use it in their prayer and conversations with the Lord. The Bible teaches that if we are praying the Word of God, which we can be certain is the will of God, we can be confident that He will hear and respond to our prayers (John 15:7). However, memorizing the scripture is not enough. If we want them to use it effectively, children need to understand what they are saying and what it means. They can't use the scripture for strength and encouragement if they do not understand it. It is not hard to explain scripture to children. Jesus Himself taught scripture to people using parables. As parents, we can do the same thing in a context our children can receive. Some of the most important scriptures are very simple in principle and easy for anyone to grasp.

Children are also more likely to share the Word of God with others when they can cite it and use it in its proper context. They become inspired to encourage their friends and associates with the same scripture you've taken the time to encourage them with.

Make a habit of quoting scripture in your daily prayers. Use scripture to encourage your kids when you talk with them about their day and during your daily check-ins with them. Find songs that include the promises of God in them. Post scriptures in your home in places where your children will be at least once a day. As I've said, the kids saw scripture on the bathroom mirror in front of where they brushed their teeth each day. These are just a few really good ways to plant the Word of God in a child's heart.

It is also important to teach godly principles in ways that encourage children to apply them all the time. A principle, by definition, is a fundamental truth that is the foundation for a belief or behavior or chain of reasoning. When we consider godly principles, we can be assured that (1) they are based in a truthful context, (2) they are consistently found throughout the Bible, (3) they do not conflict with one another, and (4) they are seen in the behavior of our Lord, Jesus Christ.

Apostle Paul writes in a letter to the believers in 2 Peter 1:3–9 (NIV),

> His divine power has given us everything we need for a godly life through our knowledge of him who called us by his own glory and goodness. Through these he has given us his very great and precious promises, so that through them you may participate in the di-

vine nature, having escaped the corruption in the world caused by evil desires. For this very reason, make every effort to add to your faith goodness; and to goodness, knowledge; and to knowledge, self-control; and to self-control, perseverance; and to perseverance, godliness; and to godliness, mutual affection; and to mutual affection, love. For if you possess these qualities in increasing measure, they will keep you from being ineffective and unproductive in your knowledge of our Lord Jesus Christ. But whoever does not have them is nearsighted and blind, forgetting that they have been cleansed from their past sins.

Teaching these principles allows our children to approach life with eyes to see and with a redemptive heart.

Love is the strongest and most dominant principle found in the Bible. And the instruction we consistently find is to love one another as we love ourselves. The Greek word "agape" means love that is unconditional, regardless of circumstance, and this is how God loves us. His love toward us is perfect. I want to love my children like God loves us. Most parents desire and intend to love their children this way, but we are not perfect at it. We don't always make the best decision when anger or selfishness gets the best of us, even when it involves our children. However, if we commit to learning about and extending love to others with an *agape type of love*, our Father, God, will be pleased.

When we are operating in love, we can see evidence of the other fruits of Spirit present in our lives. In 1 Corinthians 13, we learn what love looks like and what we must do to walk in love. I love the Message Bible's version of love:

> Love never gives up.
> Love cares more for others than for self.
> Love doesn't want what it doesn't have.
> Love doesn't strut,
> Doesn't have a swelled head,
> Doesn't force itself on others,
> Isn't always "me first,"
> Doesn't fly off the handle,
> Doesn't keep score of the sins of others,
> Doesn't revel when others grovel,
> Takes pleasure in the flowering of truth,
> Puts up with anything,

Trusts God always,

Always looks for the best,

Never looks back,

But keeps going to the end.

When we study what love looks like and translate those action words into our daily lives, we are demonstrating a humble and agape type of love. As we give love, we can be assured that we will receive it back. The Bible teaches that it never fails, it never dies. My children's first opportunities to demonstrate love involved how they treated me and one another in our home. Encouraging children to apologize and repent for actions that were not loving helps to emphasize the importance and principle of love.

Giving thanks is another act that teaches us how to live with joy, peace, and happiness. The Bible encourages us all, in both the Old and New Testament, to "be thankful," "give thanks," and "bring praises" unto the Lord. Giving thanks to the Lord is God's will for Christians. We should be thankful in all circumstances.

When children are taught to give thanks, it enables them to appreciate and respect others and discourages them from developing self-centered ways. Parents should show children that they are blessed for what they have and for what God has done in their lives. It becomes easier for children to develop a relationship with prayer, praise, and worship if they have developed a thankful heart.

The easiest way to teach a young child how to be thankful is to require them to say "please" when they are requesting something and "thank you" when it is given to them. Making a request using respectful words in nondemanding tones encourages honor, which is how we should make our requests to God in prayer. Once you provide the child with something, ask them to say "thank you" until they have learned to say it on their own. Reminding them enforces the habit and shows them it is important.

Encouraging older children to be thankful may require some additional steps. Pointing out how God has blessed them or the family is essential. When they are studying the Bible, point out how frequently we are directed to give thanks. During hard times, remind them of how God has been faithful in the past so that they can thank God for what He has done. Explain that giving thanks is one way we demonstrate to God that we love Him for who He is.

Even where there is lack, sickness, death, and sorrow, there is a place for thankfulness because we serve a merciful

God. Although it can be hard sometimes, we should not be angry with God when we are hurting or when we do not understand why something has happened. The Bible says, "For the Lord your God is a merciful God; he will not abandon or destroy you or forget the covenant with your ancestors, which he confirmed to them by oath" (Deut. 4:31 [NIV]). Reminding our children, especially teenagers, of this is important so they do not develop angry hearts when life presents difficult things. God has established a covenant with us that He will not break. That covenant is filled with promises and love, which provide us with hope. Hope is a powerful tool because it allows us to desire something with the expectation or belief that something good will happen. A bad situation will change. Because God is a good, faithful, loving God, we can be thankful that we know Him.

The fact that God is a faithful God is something we should value. The Word tells us *faith* is having confidence in what we *hope* for and assurance about what we do not see (Heb. 11:1 [NIV]). Believing that God will provide, heal, deliver, and restore is acting in faith. Our trust in God, beyond what we see, is based on our hopes and His promises.

Furthermore, a child should understand there are two parts to faith: God's part and our part. God makes a promise about something and is *faithful* to do it. He's a God that does not lie and does what He says He will do. Our part is to *believe* what He says He will do even *before* He does it.

We have a faithful God, and we live our lives believing that He is faithful. Some people refer to this as "walking by faith." That means exercising faith in the way you live your life and in the choices you make. We are walking in faith when we decide to follow His Word now and expect to see His reward later. Children can develop faith more easily than adults because they generally have not had as many challenges in their lives. However, walking by faith is not something that we teach our children once and expect them to do consistently or perfectly for the rest of their lives. Even as adults we have to remind ourselves or encourage others to live by faith. Exercising faith is a continual, ongoing decision that is strengthened by our experiences with God.

When we are exercising faith and those promises do show up, we have to diligently point them out to our children so that they see God's work at hand. Remind them of those experiences when they were hoping for or needing God in their lives and they saw how God's promises manifested. Recognition teaches them how to give praise and glory to God, a form of thanksgiving, and it also strengthens their faith.

We struggled financially in our house for many years. I did not receive financial support from their father, and so I worked two, sometimes three, jobs to keep things going. One day I was sitting on the couch looking at the electric and gas bills. Both of the bills were several months behind and had been sent with disconnection notices. It was the middle of winter, and I was trying to decide which utility was more vital to maintain. We had a gas stove and furnace, which meant we could eat and stay warm with gas, but how long could we go without electricity?

That Sunday the pastor's message was about tithing. The pastor referenced Malachi 3. The Bible compares not tithing to the act of robbing God: "You are under a curse—your whole nation—because you are robbing me" (Mal. 3:9 [NIV]). The scripture teaches that God is the same and will not change and goes on to tell us in verses 10–12 his promises to us if we tithe. God says, "Test me in this…and see if I will not throw open the floodgates of heaven and pour out so much blessing that there will not be room enough to store it."

I said to the Lord, "Your Word says to test you." As I sat there on the couch, I also remembered another scripture that I often stood on, one that states God is not a man so He cannot lie (Num. 23:19). He asks us to test Him on this point. I cried out, "Lord, I'm going to trust you and test you," but I also admitted I was scared. Tithing meant that I would not be able to pay the gas bill or the electric bill for another month. I was crying because I had no idea what the next two weeks would look like for us, but I had made the decision to trust Him. I got on the phone with both utility companies to explain that I would not be able to pay the amount due to avoid disconnection. The electric company agreed to extend the due date and allow the service to continue. The gas company asked me how much I could afford to pay monthly and set up a payment plan for that amount. When I got off the phone, my tears were no longer a sign of fear but were instead shed in thanksgiving. I was going to be able to keep both utilities and give my tithes. The following month I unexpectedly received a salary increase at work. God definitely kept His promise and proved His Word to be true!

I shared everything with the kids, even the struggle over which utility to maintain. We looked at the Malachi scripture together, especially verses 10–12, where the promises are made. I compared the changes in our lives, finances, and household to what God was promising there so they could see God's faithfulness. From that point on, I have faithfully continued to tithe and give. When the kids started working,

I asked them to trust God in this area as well. They remained disciplined in this and also saw God's blessing in their lives and finances.

As they continued to grow in their faith through their own positive experiences, they saw God's direct involvement in their lives and they became confident in God's love for them. Eventually my children began to give thanks to God on their own, without reminders from me to take the time to praise God.

In addition to the tithe, the principle of giving is important. And a child must witness their parents demonstrating the act of giving. Giving offerings and donations to others is something you must be willing to do as a parent. It is often one of those parental elements that a child needs to see rather than just hear. Luke 6:38 (NIV) says, "Give, and it will be given to you. A good measure, pressed down, shaken together and running over, will be poured into your lap. For with the measure you use, it will be measured to you." Now one interesting thing about this scripture is the awesome cyclical promise and reward that God blesses us with when we give. Although it is wonderful to celebrate with our children when God keeps His Word, they need to see us on the side of the promise wherein we are giving freely to others.

Giving, can also include the gift of time or labor; it does not always have to be a monetary gift. Giving is a value that should be practiced from childhood all the way through our adult lives. It is necessary because ultimately it is our calling as followers of Christ.

People often view good stewardship as focused only on guarding and monitoring one's money. However, in Psalm 24:1 (KJV), the Bible tells us, "The earth is the Lord's and the fullness thereof." The "fullness thereof" refers to every-thing—every blessing, gift, talent, relationship, dollar, or any other "thing" we may have. When we recognize that nothing truly belongs to us, we begin to monitor and guard what He has given us and use it all for His purpose and glory. God told Adam and Eve in the Garden of Eden to "have dominion over the fish of the sea, over the birds of the air, and over every living thing that moves on the earth" (Gen. 1:28 [NKJV]). Adam and Eve had a responsibility to oversee the entire earth, which belonged to God. Just as important as God's instruction was to Adam and Eve, His instruction to us is equally as important to accomplish for His purpose and glory.

So why is it important to teach our children this at an early age? The sooner they learn, the easier it will be for them to manage things that carry more and more responsibility as they get older. *Webster's* dictionary defines "stewardship" as "the duty or function of watching or guarding for the sake of proper direction or control." The purpose God has for our children includes gifts for them to use. They should understand how to watch and guard all that God gives. One day they will be called to use those gifts for work in the body of Christ.

Another godly principle, and a commandment of God, is to honor thy mother and father. The scripture says, "Honor your father and your mother, so that you may live long in the land the Lord your God is giving you" (Exod. 20:12 [NIV]). Honoring thy mother and father is mentioned two times in the Old Testament and four times in the New Testament. Ephesians 6:1–3 (NIV) in the New Testament states, "Children, obey your parents in the Lord, for this is right. Honor your father and mother—which is the first commandment with a promise, so that it may go well with you and that you may enjoy long life on the earth."

Honoring a parent should be a requirement in a Christian home. It should not be merely a hope or a desire. When I was growing up, a disrespectful mouth resulted in some serious ramifications. In today's society it seems that it is OK for children to tell the parent what they will or will not do even if it is the direct opposite of what a parent has instructed.

Teaching a child to obey includes emphasizing that accepting guidance from a parent identifies them as a representative of God. Honoring a parent is reflected in appreciation and acknowledgment that obedience and discipline develop into wisdom.

In addition to the responsibility of teaching our children about honoring thy mother and father, Ephesians 6:4 (AMP) goes on to instruct, "Fathers, do not provoke your children to anger [do not exasperate them to the point of resentment with demands that are trivial or unreasonable or humiliating or abusive, nor by showing favoritism or indifference to any of them], but bring them up [tenderly, with lovingkindness] in the discipline and instruction of the Lord." If we want our children to follow God's command, we should also follow God's specific instruction here on raising our children.

Teaching Children How to Pray

It probably goes without saying that there are certain things we definitely intend to teach our children—for example, a three-generation family recipe for macaroni and cheese or chocolate-chip cake (those are my favorites!). But one thing that should also be intentionally taught is how to pray.

As parents, we should assure that praying begins when they are in the womb, before they are born. As they get older, they will observe the time you've set aside for praying with them in the morning, before meals, and in the evenings before bed. As their speech develops, they can join in with commonly used words like "Thank you," "Jesus," and "Amen!" The point is to have your child acknowledge that praying is something we do in this house.

As kids develop in their knowledge of the ABCs and 123s, they should also be learning prayers that are easy to remember and recite. A commonly taught prayer for many children before each meal is "God is grace; God is good. Let us thank Him for our food. By His hands, we all are fed. Thank you, Lord, for our daily bread." It is amazing to see children nowadays as young as two and three operating mobile devices. As such, it should totally be expected that they are able to learn to pray and participate in prayer!

As a teenager, I had memorized the Lord's prayer and prayed it once a week. The church I grew up in recited the prayer weekly during the service, as many churches do. Unfortunately it took me a while to realize that in my private prayer time, I could talk to Him about so much more. Certainly, God will honor the Lord's prayer, just as it is written, because He is a faithful God. What I didn't realize when I was a teenager was that the Lord's prayer is about how Jesus was teaching the disciples to pray. When they ask Him how to pray, he says in Matthew 6:9–15 (KJV) to do this:

> Our Father, who art in heaven,
> hallowed be thy Name,
> thy kingdom come,
> thy will be done,
> on earth as it is in heaven.
> Give us this day our daily bread.
> And forgive us our trespasses,
> as we forgive those
> who trespass against us.
> And lead us not into temptation,
> but deliver us from evil.
> For thine is the kingdom,
> and the power, and the glory,
> for ever and ever.
> Amen.

The opening of the prayer—"Our Father in heaven, hallowed be that name"—is a recognition and praise of who God is and where He reigns and a declaration that we shall worship His name. When we invite God's "kingdom to come as it is in heaven," we are opening our hearts and minds to His will and inviting His authority into our lives here on earth. "Give us this day, our daily bread" is a request for His provision, which can be read both spiritually as His wisdom and literally as pertaining to our physical needs. The prayer directs us to repent of our sins and declare we will forgive others and also teaches us to ask for God to help us forgo temptation and "deliver us from evil." These things help us acknowledge that we are sinners who need God's help and remind us of the importance of forgiveness. They help us recognize we as sinners are coming to our Holy Father and placing our requests at His throne. Finally, the prayer ends with an acclamation of faith that His kingdom, which we are putting our trust and requests before, is powerful and glorious forever.

I believe the key elements in this prayer that should be included in all my prayers, whether I am reciting the Lord's Prayer or not, are (1) recognition of the Father and His authority, (2) praise and worship of the Father, (3) submission of my will to His will, (4) my prayer requests, (5) deliverance from sin, (6) repentance and forgiveness of sin, and (7) a declaration of my faith. I believe this is the instruction given to us by Jesus on how to pray.

For example, if I pray the following simple, short prayer for my children, I can include these elements and be confident that I have prayed the way Jesus instructed me to pray.

> Dear Father, I honor and worship you as the Alpha (beginning) and Omega (end). I ask that you lead me and provide me with all that I need to be the parent you desire me to be. Please forgive me for anything that does not align with your Word. I put my trust in you and believe that you hear my prayers and will answer them. Amen.

Praying with my children and including these elements in our prayers, I believe, taught them to pray in a simple and fearless manner.

I believe the most effective, well-rounded way to pray is to consistently declare scripture for specific areas you seek God's authority and provision in. One of the simplest promises in the Bible is *Jesus loves me*. That promise is included in a song that many children learn early, which says, "Jesus loves me, this I know, for the Bible tells me so." The lyrics include two very important pieces of information for the child to remember. First, the child is confirming that Jesus loves them. Secondly, they know this is true because the Bible says so. They have an early understanding of a promise from God and where to go to find the promise.

Prayers with Promise

There are promises all throughout the Bible, and they address everything we need. There are scriptures that tell us what to do when we are feeling confused, discouraged, lonely, or afraid. The Word of God directs us what to do when we are tempted by the enemy, sick, or financially struggling. God's promises also speak to us specifically about our faith and His strength, love, eternity, grace, and mercy.

Most parents want to be able to provide for all of their children's needs all of the time. However, the reality is that we don't always have the ability to provide because sometimes we don't even know what they need. Not even the wealthiest parent can provide everything a child needs because not every need is material. The Bible tells us that. God does know everything we need before we need it because of His almighty, omnipotent power (Matt. 6:8 [NIV]).

There are lots of resources available in print and online that enable quick and easy access to scripture about the promises of God. Some books compile the promises and sort the scriptures by subject or "need" so they can be found quickly. Although I have several Bibles in my home, I have always enjoyed having these types of books around for quick reference and as a tool to use for Bible study. I also keep extra "promise books" on hand as these make awesome gifts to share.

Referencing God's promises shows us how He wants us to live and how He wants to bless us. He wants us to know the Lord is a Savior, Deliverer, Provider, Protector, and Healer. Knowing this, our children can go boldly to the Lord with their requests. These scriptures identify how we should behave or what we should choose and then go on to explain what God will do in return, even though we may not deserve it. God is not asking us to do something to earn these blessings. He is asking us to follow His wisdom and guidance. The instruction for us is to do something simple, founded on our choice to believe in who He is. One example is 1 John 1:9 (NIV), which says, "If we confess our sins, He is faithful and just and will forgive us our sins and purify us from all unrighteousness." Another example can be seen in Matthew 7:7 (NKJV): "*Ask* and it will be given to you; seek and you will find; knock and the door will be opened to you." If we recognize that God is holy and confess that we are sinners, then He will faithfully forgive us and purify us.

Promise scriptures are full of wisdom. If we are teaching God's instruction and guidance to our children through His scripture, we can be confident we are teaching action that is good and wise and that the promises of God will manifest in their lives.

Promise scriptures to share:

Exodus 20:12

Honor your father and your mother, so that you may live long.

Isaiah 46:10

All My plans will be fulfilled, for I know the end from the beginning.

Matthew 21:22

If you believe in Me, you will receive whatever you ask for in prayer.

Proverbs 3:5–6

Trust in Me with all your heart and I will guide you.

Ephesians 6:11

My armor will help you stand against the plans of the enemy.

Isaiah 64:4

If you wait for Me, I will work on your behalf.

Hebrews 11:6

I will reward those who diligently seek Me with a heart of faith.

1 Corinthians 13:8

My love will never fail you.

Isaiah 54:13

I will teach your children My ways and give them great peace.

Romans 8:31

If I am for you, no one can stand against you.

Declarative Prayer

Leading children in declarative prayer can help them know that they are loved. They are declaring scriptures about who God says we are and what we can do. These scriptures by nature are intended to build us up and give us confidence in the love God has for us.

Encourage children to speak the words and not just listen to you read them. Try having them replace the pronoun in the scripture with their own name. That way the child is claiming the scriptures as their own for their life. Speaking God's Word out loud brings declarative power that is amazing and shows us how the Spirit of God will fill us up with joy and strength. His Word says, "You will also declare a thing, and it will be established for you" (Job 22:28 [KJV]). Whatever we don't want we have the authority to reject, and whatever we desire we have the authority to establish in our lives. Since we are believers, our mouths are our weapons for deliverance, our weapons for change, our weapons for bringing supernatural transformation to our lives spiritually and physically in Jesus's name.

Declarative prayer statements to share:

Deuteronomy 28:26

I declare I am blessed coming in and blessed going out.

Ephesians 6:10

I declare I am strong in the Lord and in the power of His might.

Romans 8:17

I declare I am an heir of God and a joint heir with Jesus Christ.

Philippians 4:19

I declare God will supply all my needs according to His riches in Christ.

1 Corinthians 2:16

I declare I have the mind of Christ.

2 Corinthians 5:7

I declare I am walking by faith and not by sight.

Psalms 146:2

I declare I will praise the Lord all my life and sing praises to Him as long as I live.

Isaiah 53:5

I declare I am healed by the stripes of Jesus.

Luke 10:19

I declare I have authority over the enemy.

Romans 8:28

I declare all things work together for my good because I love Him.

When the children grew older, I started taking a public train to work so they dropped me off and drove themselves to school. But we still prayed. Every morning. We talked very plainly about what was going on in our lives and ended our prayers with very familiar scriptures. We included a request for a hedge of protection to surround us by the blood of Jesus and a promise that we would "dwell in the secret place of most High God and abide under the shadow of the Almighty" (Ps. 91:1 [KJV]).

The children learned how to pray and understood that it wasn't complicated. They learned that it did not need to be formal. Eventually we all started taking turns leading the morning prayers. I believe it is extremely important for children to sometimes be the leader in prayer with their families because it teaches them to overcome doubt about knowing how to pray. It also enables them to learn to pray for others and incorporate the needs of other people into their prayers.

We prayed specifically about problems, challenges, and new things we encountered. When someone was sick, we prayed for healing and restoration in their life. The kids were pretty active in sports and performing arts, so we prayed before games and performances. Our prayers also included requests for God to show us how to exercise discipline and self-control in our lives.

The more we prayed together, the more comfortable they felt speaking to the Lord about their lives. They were developing their own relationship with the Lord.

As we talk to the Lord in prayer, the Holy Spirit will lead us and guide us. The more we work at forging a stronger relationship with God, the better we become at hearing the voice of God speak to us in our prayer time. As a parent, I was able to watch the kids grow in that area. Their prayers grew to include worship and thanksgiving. They began to seek wisdom and direction to go boldly to the throne of God with their prayer requests.

Inviting the Joy of the Lord

The ability to invite the joy of the Lord is essential because when the presence of the Lord is among you and your family, you will be amazed at what can happen. The Bible tells us where two or three gather in the Lord's name, there shall He also be (Matt. 18:20 [NIV]). The joy of the Lord can overcome sorrow, restore peace, encourage thanksgiving, invoke praise, and lead us and guide us.

Inviting the joy of the Lord should come with an understanding that Jesus Himself has to be the source of your life. Jesus bore our sins, and died on the cross for our sins, so that we could be redeemed. This is what the joy of the Lord brings us—the ability to enjoy the freedom He has given us through victory and redemption. Receiving Jesus and recognizing that He is the sole source of joy are the first steps.

While there are many relationships, things, and activities we can enjoy, recognizing that true fulfillment comes through the joy of the Lord is critical to understanding our children's happiness.

Edifying the Lord so that He can be there with us, as He says, means praying and singing and giving praise and thanksgiving to the Lord every opportunity we have to do it. I love to sing and listen to music, and I would say 95 percent of the music we play in our home and car is praise and worship music. I had my favorites, which my children would see and hear me dance to all the time. I would invite them to join in with me all the time. As I mentioned, we invited the Lord to be with us each morning and asked the angels in heaven to guard over us and the blood of Jesus to protect us. We were constantly seeking ways to magnify Christ and invite Him to be with us regularly.

I've also spoken before about how important Philippians 4:13 is to us and how that one scripture was such an important stepping stone in my children's lives, all the way through adulthood. Not only does it encourage and strengthen one for whatever comes, but it is a magnification of who Jesus is.

Another favorite scripture was "Trust in the LORD with all thine heart; And lean not unto thine own understanding. In all thy ways acknowledge him, And he shall direct thy paths" (Proverbs 3:5–6 [KJV]). Encouraging the kids in this

was common practice in our house because I wanted them to be confident in inviting the Lord into their lives and acknowledging and trusting God and how He guides us.

Choosing to invite the Lord into your relationship with your children should be personal and specific to you and your children. As a single mother, I always wanted the three of us to feel special to each other. Therefore Ecclesiastes 4:11–12 (NIV) became yet another favorite of ours. The scripture says, "Also, if two lie down together, they will keep warm. But how can one keep warm alone? Though one may be overpowered, two can defend themselves. A cord of three strands is not quickly broken." It was special to us because it represented that a three-cord strand is not easily broken if the strands strengthen one another. This is how we viewed our relationship amongst the three of us. When I read the scripture, it always reminded me of the trinity in God the Father, God the Son, and God the Spirit. We invited the trinity of God to dwell in the midst of our three-cord strand. This bond meant so much to us.

ME AND MY HOUSE

Serving the Lord

In Joshua 24:15(NIV), Joshua gathers the tribes of Israel and says, "If it is unacceptable in your sight to serve the Lord, choose for yourselves this day whom you will serve: whether the gods which your fathers served that were on the other side of the River, or the gods of the Amorites in whose land you live; but as for me and my house, we will serve the Lord." Just as Joshua did, I have always chosen that "me and my house shall serve the Lord"!

Having a house that served the Lord meant getting up and going to church every Sunday, but it also meant participating in ministry groups and being involved in Bible study. Regardless of the children's age, participation and involvement in ministry and fellowship were required.

Attending church was ingrained in me as a child growing up in my grandparents' house. While I do not know how many generations ago that was required, I do know it was a precedent set with my grandparent's children. No matter what had happened the day before or how busy life got or how tired we were from the night before, church was a permanent-red-marker appointment on the calendar!

I never realized until I had children how important establishing that precedence in the home is. Committing consistently to engaging in praise and worship with other believers shows your children that fellowship should be an important part of their lives. It shows them that church is just as important as school. Don't get me wrong, worship in the house is important, but how God instructs us to fellowship with other believers is important as well.

I grew up in an old Southern church where we went to Sunday School, which was as close to Bible study as we had back then, and it was divided into three sections—children, young adults, and adults. After Sunday School was over, the regular service began and the children returned to the main sanctuary to sit quietly in the seat next to their families during the service. The problem was that no message was really being taught other than the traditional message that "saints go to heaven; sinners go to hell." "Serving the Lord" meant joining the usher board, working in the kitchen ministry, or becoming a choir member, deacon, or deaconess. While these ministries are important, they became more of a venue for carrying out religious traditions than a conduit through which one realized the privilege or honor of serving the Lord.

I remember as a kid sitting in the church pews still and quiet and staring at the pastor while he spoke, yet I had no idea what he was saying. One Sunday when I was about sixteen years old, the pastor said something that I related to, and he caught my ear. I began seeking the meaning of that message, but it was still a challenge to leave most services with any understanding.

Churches nowadays tend to hold more child and young adult ministries, as well as classes taught during the regular service. I knew that I wanted my children to participate in those ministries so they would not sit in the service with me uninvolved and deprived of understanding. It was also important for me to know that the youth ministries were teaching and ministering rather than just babysitting. I wanted to know that my children were really taking part in a message of God. I felt comfortable when they could tell me what they had learned and discussed in Children's Church.

Discipline versus Obedience

Discipline and obedience are often used interchangeably; however, there is a difference between the two. Obedience is instruction or command that is given, followed by an action performed. Discipline is behavior chosen because it is right, whether a person has been told to do it or not. Discipline evolves into wisdom and self-control. The development of discipline and self-control is a result of obedience (or training).

Developing discipline and requiring obedience are difficult because they speak directly to our will as human beings. Young or old, a child wants to rebel against your word and the Word of God and walk in their own way. We can all say that we struggle with discipline and obedience.

However, the Bible instructs us many times to discipline our children as God disciplines us and to observe the commands of the Lord (Deut. 8:5–6 [NIV]). We can reasonably conclude that the portion of the scripture that says, "Observe the commands" points to demonstrating obedience. As parents, we are warned that if we do not require discipline and obedience, we lead them astray. As grown adults, both of my children have come to me individually and actually thanked me for being as strict as I was with discipline and obedience as requirements for godly behavior in our home. That was because as they got older, they could see the effects of a lack of discipline and obedience on people their age with different problems and negative circumstances. What a wonderful blessing it was to hear both of them tell me that they appreciated me for this. I give all the glory to God for that!

No one enjoys discipline all of the time while they are in the midst of it—especially not children—because it means we are controlling something we want to do, whether it is good or bad. It can mean suppressing a desire or submitting to authority, whether we are forced to do it or not. For a parent, training your children to be disciplined and enforcing punishment when they don't obey requires effort and consistency. However, we can be assured, according to the Bible, "it produces a harvest of righteousness and peace for those who have been trained by it" (Heb. 12:11 [NIV]).

Training a child to be obedient requires establishing rules that align with the Word of God. It is not the parent's role to be their child's friend. That's not to say that a parent and child shouldn't enjoy doing things together or having the same interests or being able to share things with one another as friends do. However, there should also be boundaries between a parent and a child where the child understands the authority of the parent. Making friends with a child in lieu of requiring obedience yields no reward if the child destroys their life or someone else's life in the long term.

Explaining to the child why they should obey and how this aligns with scripture is important, but even if the child doesn't understand the rule or disagrees with it, the child should still be expected to follow it. One simple way to explain this is to state that a lack of obedience, lack of self-control and lack of discipline is not pleasing to God.

The Word of God gives us plenty of guidance on how to discipline our children. In Proverbs 3:11 (NIV) and Hebrews 12:4–11(NIV), the Word refers to the Lord's discipline and the Lord's rebuke. The scriptures tell us not to resent or be upset with God when we are disciplined or rebuked because He does so towards the ones He loves. The Hebrew word for discipline is *yasar*, meaning a form of corrective action or circumstance. The word for rebuke in Hebrew is *yakach*, which means to make a decision with words. Through the repeated use of these words in the Bible, one meaning to enforce with actions and the other to enforce with words, we see both are clearly important to God.

In some situations the use of both words and consequential actions is needed. Indeed, sometimes it is not enough to only correct a child with words. Have you ever heard that phrase "It seems like my words go in one ear and out the other?" This refers to the fact that a child has the ability to hear the words you are speaking but sometimes does not receive them well enough to change their behavior.

Society has developed opinions and judgments about whether discipline for a child should include spanking. But the Bible instructs us that the rod and reprimand are acceptable and advises that punishment with the rod should not be withheld (Prov. 29:15 [NIV] and Prov. 23:13–14 [NIV]). I love what the Message version of the Bible says, "Don't be afraid to correct your young ones; a spanking won't kill them. A good spanking, in fact, might save them from something worse than death" (Prov. 23:13 [MSG]).

When I was a child, there was no debate about "sparing the rod" in my grandparents' house. I received plenty of spankings. Spankings were given by hand, brush, belt, shoe—whatever was closest. But what could be referred to as the "*real* rod" was the one I hated the most. It was what my grandmother called a switch. Switches are thin, weed-like branches pulled from a tree or bush. I would often be sent outside to pick the switch I was subsequently going to be punished with and bring it back to my grandmother for my spanking. It was a long walk to pick out a switch and return to the house. It certainly gave me enough time to think about my actions.

As a parent, I never spanked my children with switches or other objects, but I did spank my children on their bottoms with my hand so they would understand that certain behavior would not be tolerated.

Discipline and obedience should begin early and continue, from the time children first engage in defiance all the way through adolescence and until they leave the home. Establishing rules that train the child against defiant behavior can begin when a child throws a temper tantrum, hits another sibling or person, or does something they were told not to do. Beginning to discipline a child at this age is a lot easier than trying to discipline a teen who has not consistently been taught the consequences of disobedience.

When you are consistent and do not compromise with these boundaries, you are effectively disciplining your children. It is also extremely critical that both parents are not only consistent but also committed to the established rules. It does absolutely no good for one parent to be the "good cop" and the other parent to be the "bad cop." One parent who consistently compromises or refrains from enforcing the consequence of misbehavior destroys the boundaries in a home. Children will catch on to that very quickly and learn how to manipulate the system. While it is OK for one parent to be the enforcer, the other parent must show the child that they fully agree with disciplinary words and actions.

Making sure that the enforcement of godly behavior is effective and appropriate is key. For example, if the consequence for a teenager is to be grounded and unable to leave the home and hang out with friends, don't allow the child to continue communication through social media on a cell phone or computer. Assuming the purpose of the punishment is to prevent the child from engaging in entertainment with friends, if they are still doing that through social media, no effective punishment has been enforced. If the internet is required for school or work-related activities, take the time to monitor their use of the tool so that it is only used for completion of the work.

The godly purpose of discipline and obedience is to lead a child to submit to God and His commandments because they desire to please God and do what is right. God's promise and reward are that they may walk in wisdom and live a blessed life. Discipline and obedience are also demonstrations of love to us by our Lord and to our children as parents.

Responsibility to Pray

Remember, earlier we acknowledged that children are gifts from God. Therefore, praying for our children, on their behalf, is also a huge responsibility that we must be diligent in. Praying daily, with purpose and in detail with regard to every area of our child's life, is critical. Declaring God's Word all over their lives helped reassure me that I was meeting the responsibility of being a good praying parent.

Even today I pray for my adult children in specific areas of their lives that I started praying about when they were children. I remember specifically praying for my children to love God and to have a relationship with God independent of my relationship with Him. I prayed for them to have godly friends and mentors, stay attracted to a God-centered life, and grow in their faith. I began praying for the spouses God had specifically chosen for them—unless it was His will for them to remain single. My children are young adults now, but I began praying these prayers when they were in elementary school.

These are just a few of the areas in which I consistently prayed for my children. There are so many more things you can request and proclaim for your children in prayer. God will be so faithful to provide. When I look back at some of the prayers and requests I made when they were small children, I can clearly see evidence of God's answered prayers in their lives today. God does answer prayer!

Godly Home

As our children grow older, controlling what comes in and out of the house is vital. I do recognize how much more difficult it is today than it was twenty years ago. However, a parent's diligence in monitoring what their children are exposed to is extremely important, regardless of today's technology. We have power in our Lord, for he says, "I have told you these things, so that in me you may have peace. In this world you will have trouble. But take heart! I have overcome the world" (John 16:33 [NIV]). Ultimately, God has control over every cell phone!

I believe the most significant area of ungodly exposure is what a parent allows to be brought into the home rather than what a child is exposed to outside of the house. Swearing or offensive language, provocative behavior, or violent or demonic themes can cause more harm than one may think. A parent, without too much effort, can tell a child no if the child requests to participate in something outside the home the parent views as ungodly. For example, if the child requests to go to the house of someone who regularly displays ungodly behavior, it is easy for a parent to say no. Or the parent can disallow the child from participating in an activity the parent views as wrong. That's not to say that a child cannot disobey when they are outside of the house, but for the most part, a parent can regulate where a child goes and subsequently what the child does.

However, it requires way more effort to regulate what ungodly things are brought into the home because of how accessible ungodly entertainment and influences can be through social media, television, and the internet. A parent might make the assumption that because the child is at home, nothing wrong is going on. Often a parent will excuse the responsibility of regulating what is happening in the home because of the amount of diligence and prayer that is required to monitor what children are exposed to in the home. What is allowed in a home is a choice.

For example, just because a large percentage of entertainment (TV, music, and movies) includes ungodly and negative influences does not mean that we have to allow our children to engage in it. When my children were young, a very popular cartoon frequently represented the child being disrespectful to the parents. After noticing the pattern, I did not allow my children to watch it again. It was ungodly behavior that I did not want my children to believe was acceptable. I continue to be amazed when I see the level of disrespect for authority in our schools, businesses, and families. Modern media idolizes these themes and concepts, but when we allow it in our homes, we are essentially confirming that disobedience, ungodliness, and disrespect are OK.

Regulation of good entertainment in a Christian home is not impossible. Negative entertainment can be replaced in your home with wholesome entertainment. It provides an opportunity for you to expose children to live performing arts, musicals, and older music that was not centered around sex. There is Christian contemporary music children can enjoy that praises and worships God. Having a broader range of entertainment will widen their appreciation for art.

When I thought the kids were old enough, I allowed them to have cell phones. Monitoring exactly what they were doing at all times was difficult, but I did find some things to do to help. I paid attention to how often they were on the phone when they should have been doing other things. I insisted they view the phone as a privilege, not a necessity. So if I felt like they were not following the rules in an area, I simply took the phone away. I set timers on the phone through my service provider to prevent usage after a certain time in the evening. I did this all the way through their high school years, despite the fact that none of their friends' parents had put any usage restrictions on their phones. Whether it was the "norm" or not did not affect the rules in my house. The rules and limits set a standard and expectation for children that says holiness is a priority in the house.

As I said, I do understand there are challenges that are present now that were not here twenty years ago, or even ten years ago. However, I still believe that a parent can consistently monitor what their children are doing, who they are following or who is following them, and how much time they are spending on social media or participating in other ungodly acts.

Godly Friends

Maintaining a godly home provides children with an attraction to like-minded people. Holiness attracts holiness, and we can pray for God's grace and mercy that our children always be centered around godly people. The Bible says in Proverbs 13:20 (NKJV), "He who walks with wise men will be wise, but the companion of fools will be destroyed."

I believe when my kids left for college, they were eager to experience life on their own but were immediately introduced to a culture of life that conflicted with the rules in my house. They were in a community of people who were not godly and not as hungry to grow in their relationships with God. They became more and more uncomfortable, but eventually God enabled them to develop better relationships with other believers. When my daughter began to work as a missionary, she met people all over the country who participated with her in those missions. She still enjoys spending time with them. She recently told me that fellowshipping with like-minded Christian friends brings life to her and is worth the travel time it takes to visit those friends.

The children have also maintained long-term friendships with godly people and role models they met when they were much younger. Connecting with these lifelong friends has enabled all of them to see how God has worked in one another's lives over the years.

Godly Behavior

Instilling the importance of holiness and purity in our children's lives enables them to not only attract other people who are holy and pure but also to be an example for those who are not.

The Bible says in 1 Thessalonians 4:7 (NIV), "for God did not call us to be impure, but to live a holy life." In Matthew 5:8 (NIV), the Bible says, "Blessed are the pure at heart, for they shall see God." We want our children to understand that God does expect us to carry ourselves in a certain way that reflects who we are in Him. He wants us to demonstrate His laws in how we live our lives. The Bible also says, "Let no one despise your youth, but be an example to the believers in word, in conduct, in love, in spirit, in faith, in purity" (1 Tim. 4:12 [NKJV]).

How we speak, dress, behave, and the like are all reflections of a holy life or, conversely, can represent an unclean life. My grandmother did not allow me to dress provocatively, even if we disagreed on what provocative dressing looked like. I never told her that I disagreed with her (that would have ended badly for me); I just had to keep changing my outfit until I found one she thought was decent. The point is that she considered how you dressed an invitation to what (or who) you would attract to your life. Looking back, I totally agree.

I also think the mindset that says, "They will encounter it sooner or later" is wrong and should be rebuked by a parent for their child. This mindset supports the lie that working hard to encourage holiness and purity is pointless and does no good.

Ungodly thinking says, "What's the point if we know that our children will be introduced to a secular culture anyway?" Through prayer, we can overcome temptations of the world (1 Cor. 10:13 [NIV]). *And* with the Word of God and the power of the Holy Spirit, we are equipped for spiritual warfare.

According to Ephesians 6:10–12 (NIV), we are to "be strong in the Lord and in his mighty power. Put on the full armor of God, so that you can take your stand against the devil's schemes. For our struggle is not against flesh and blood, but against the rulers, against the authorities, against the powers of this dark world and against the spiritual forces of evil in the heavenly realms." The gospel books of the Bible—Matthew, Mark, Luke, and John—all include scripture documenting Jesus's time with the disciples. The term "Christlike manner" has been developed because chapters in these books demonstrate how Jesus behaved and responded to people in all situations. The Bible even says that Jesus was tempted like a man but overcame the temptations by praying and speaking the written Word. We can apply this same type of behavior in our lives.

Our prayers should be that when our children find themselves in a situation where temptation or ungodly things are presented, they are prompted by the Holy Spirit to turn away from it, that they remain led by the Spirit to say no to invitations that are not holy or pure.

This is not a prayer that ends when they leave home. It is a prayer we want to continue for our children throughout their lives. If a child does get offtrack, we can commit to faithfully praying that they will turn back to the Lord with a willing spirit to remain holy and pure.

I had the "sex talk" with both of my children when my daughter was in third grade, and they learned about menstrual cycles. I believed that if they were old enough to understand why girls had menstrual cycles and boys did not, they were old enough to talk about sex. Having waited until they were attracted to the opposite sex, in my opinion, would have certainly been too late.

Talking about sex allowed us to openly discuss why sex outside of marriage, sexual immorality, and unhealthy relationships were wrong. I could explain that a healthy relationship between a man and woman should line up with how the Bible views holiness.

Movies and music that idolized sexual immorality were also not allowed, especially when they got older and could understand why it was not pure. The kids were actively involved in healthy activities outside of the home so they were rarely home alone. There were very few opportunities for them to invite unsupervised guests into our home and subsequently set up an opportunity for ungodly behavior to occur.

The goal was not to teach them that sex was bad, and I do not believe I did so. The children were adults when I got married to their stepfather. While making plans for the wedding, my daughter asked me if we would be going to a hotel for the night. I was curious why she was asking about a hotel since we were not planning to go on a honeymoon right away. So, I asked, "What do you mean?". She must have noticed the reaction on my face because she said, "Mom, I know what you will be doing. It's what the Bible says you should be doing!"

The Bible warns us throughout about succumbing to flesh and allowing our minds and bodies to control our lives. The use of drugs and alcohol is one way of doing this. It says, "if you are living according to the flesh, you are going to die. But if by the Spirit you are habitually putting to death the sinful deeds of the body, you will live" (Rom. 8:13 [AMP]).

Any type of drug, whether it is prescribed or not, alters or controls the body in some way. When a doctor prescribes the drug, there is an evaluation of how the body responds to see if it controls the problem without negatively affecting other parts of the body. When alcohol and drugs are used with the intention of providing pleasure solely to our flesh, we are giving our mind and body, rather than our spirit, control.

Drugs and alcohol and other addictions like smoking put our children in negative situations or environments that can lead to physical injury, mental suffering, financial trouble, and poor relationships. Even if our children are not using these things themselves, they can nonetheless find themselves in an environment in which others are doing it. No parent wants to see their child suffer, even if they themselves are bound by their own addictions.

Jesus tells us in John 10:10 (NKJV) that "The thief [Satan] comes only to steal and kill and destroy; I have come that they may have life, and have it to the full." In terms of addictions, the enemy's strategy to "steal, kill, and destroy" can easily be seen. An addiction can *steal* your desire to allow the Holy Spirit to lead you past your fleshly temptations and instead make you believe you need the addictive element. The fact that smoking or the use of drugs or alcohol can literally *kill* a person in many different ways is evident. An addiction can *destroy* your life because it affects every area of your life, including your relationships, jobs, purpose, and work in the body of Christ. However, the Bible says we have been given the authority over the enemy (Luke 10:19 [NIV]). The scripture also says in John 10:10 (NIV), that an abundant life means a full, complete, and plentiful one. Through Him, we *receive* the Spirit, and He *heals* our bodies and *restores* our blessings. Praise the Lord!

It is never too early to begin praying that your child will not be held captive to these things—drugs, alcohol, smoking, or any other addiction. We don't know when they might be exposed to those things or even how they might be affected by someone else's addiction. We can pray they have an abundant life, dependent on Christ and not on these substances. As they grow older, we can pray that our children have the strength by the Holy Spirit to say no and avoid the temptation when it is presented and that if our children ever become bound by an addiction, they will be delivered from it and turn their life back toward God.

Additionally, if we want our children to avoid the temptation of drugs, alcohol, smoking, and so on offered by others, we certainly can't be responsible for exposing it to them. Bringing those things into your home not only means your kids will see you use them and will likely repeat the pattern in their own lives but also that they have access to them. A child may not even recognize what the purpose of the substance is, but access to it encourages curiosity about the use of it.

It was medically discovered that smoking can negatively affect people's bodies, even if the affected person is not the person smoking. This is called secondhand smoke and when it is inhaled it can cause harm. So some smokers believe that going outside to smoke will alleviate the problem by protecting children from secondhand smoke. However, there is still the issue of the addiction and the bondage it represents. The same is true for alcohol. A small child wonders, "Why do my parents drink things all the time that I am not allowed to drink?" This is an example set in the home by the parent.

There is also a mindset out there that "healthy" or "occasional" use is OK. That can be true. But if you view smoking for years as being healthy and not representing an addiction, that is a lie. The need to have an alcoholic drink every night is an addiction. "Addiction" is defined as a strong and harmful need to regularly have something or do something. Preventing the use of drugs, alcohol, and smoking in our homes helps our children see that acquiring joy and peace are never dependent on these things.

Effectively Nosy

One thing my children had to learn (and accept) was that I was going to be nosy! Some people call it nagging, but I prefer to call it "effectively nosy with the intent to love."

It's OK to be nosy about our children's lives, but there is an effective way to do it and an ineffective way to do it. If we consistently inquire about the details of their lives, what they are doing and thinking, and how they feel about things, we can pray specifically for those areas of their lives. We can pray they progress in the positive things and encourage them. We can also discourage them from mindsets that do not align with the Word of God, as well as things that may cause them harm. This is being effectively nosy.

If a parent is interested in these details of their child's life but doesn't expand on the conversation and show interest, confirm their love for the child, or offer any encouragement or wisdom, I believe the interest is ineffective. Additionally, if you are only using the children's accomplishments to boast about them outside the home to others or share information that convinces others to pay special attention to them, your interest is based in pride. Your interest should be genuine and intended to demonstrate your love to them.

Many places in the Word show us how God the Father cares about the details of our lives. One of my favorites is Luke 12:7 (NIV): "Indeed, the very hairs of your head are all numbered. Don't be afraid; you are worth more than many sparrows." Another scripture says, "'For I know the plans I have for you,' declares the Lord, 'plans to prosper you and not to harm you, plans to give you hope and a future'" (Jer. 29:11 [NIV]).

He also shows us what He will do for us and provides the wisdom we need to live our lives. We can pray to God and ask Him to give us wisdom about how to effectively seek details of our children's lives with love.

So how do you do it? How do you stay engaged without driving your children crazy? You have to ask questions! Some people are just naturally inquisitive, and so it will be easy, but others are not. For those who are not naturally nosy, admittedly, you will have to work harder. But just know it will become easier.

I think there is an incorrect assumption that the "How was your day?" question is enough to show interest in a loved one's life. Let me address that now—it's not! Most of the time, our daily activities are the same. We go to work; our kids go to school and maybe soccer practice. That's the norm, and so most of the time, the response to "How was your day?" is "It was OK." Unless there is a major exchange of communication, details of the day don't usually get shared. This is true in our relationships with our children, our marriages, and our relationships with siblings.

The reason it becomes easier to engage in inquisitive dialogue with your loved ones is that when you learn about the details of your child's life, you can follow up on those areas. You can display your love by expressing your concerns, and offering your guidance and assistance. Here's an example of how a simple conversation full of questions for your child can promote these things.

> PARENT: "Hey, how was your day?"
> CHILD: "It was OK."
> PARENT: "What new things did you learn today?"
> CHILD: "We are working on stuff for this math test."
> PARENT: "When is it?"
> CHILD: "Friday."
> PARENT: "Do you feel OK about the test?"

CHILD: "Yeah, I guess."

PARENT: "What is the test on?"

CHILD: "I don't know…some stuff that makes no sense to me"

PARENT: "Hey. I know what you mean—I was never a genius in math either. Let's take a look at it together and see if I can help."

This brief conversation demonstrates how the parent's questions and concerns enabled the child to talk about their day in detail and revealed that the child was confused and discouraged. This conversation allowed the parent to offer one-on-one guidance and encouragement that said, "You're not the only one who has ever been confused" and the opportunity to pray for the child later. None of that would have come with a conversation that ended with "It was OK."

I can say that our evenings were busy all of the time when the kids were younger. Our schedules in the evenings meant I needed to cook a quick thirty-minute meal and get it on the table. I would often have the kids come into the kitchen with me and talk to me while I was cooking. While I was turned toward the stove, I was asking my questions and listening to their responses. If I heard a mood or tone change that sounded negative, it prompted me to stop what I was doing and turn to my child with full attention. The point is the opportunity to sit down face-to-face in a perfect, noise-free environment to talk with a child daily may not always be realistic. But that does not mean that you cannot be an active listener. Even in the midst of doing things, a parent can still ask questions and engage in a conversation and listen with interest. However, if you're watching TV or using your cell phone, it's a little harder to be an active listener or effectively nosy because you are likely listening to someone else's conversation or focused on information about something else. Listening with attention means you're aware of your child's body language, tone, and mood.

When the kids were in elementary school, they couldn't wait to tell me about their days and followed me around the house with details. When they entered the preteen and teen stages, the percentage of times they *volunteered* information declined. If I didn't seek it, they were not going to offer it. Oftentimes what they said did not represent the reality of a situation. They tended to internalize everything and attempt to focus on other things. Even when they were watching TV, playing a video game, or scrolling on a phone, I still checked in. As long as they were answering my detailed questions, I never required eye contact either unless there was a disciplinary action or apology needed. I viewed that level of attention as an act of respect with an acknowledgment from them that whatever the issue was, it would not happen again.

I will admit, sometimes during a Q and A session I got an "OMG, Mom" or an "*Ugh!*" but when all of that was done, I still got a response to my questions. How they felt about my "effectively nosy with the intent to love" efforts never offended me. Understanding what was going on in my children's lives was far more important!

We should also not be afraid to ask our children questions we feel they may be uncomfortable answering. Some parents believe they will hurt their children if they ask them to talk about their problems or fears and so avoid discussing such things with them. However, the Bible says, "The fear of human opinion disables; trusting in God protects you from that." (Prov. 29:25 [MSG]). Our own fear of how our children will feel prevents us from trusting in God and allowing Him to lead us in helping our children. We have to pray that God will show us how to help our children through the power of the Holy Spirit and encourage them to trust God.

An Active House

Working two and three jobs and completing my bachelor's and master's degrees meant I had to actively engage in lots of work late in the evening, sometimes overnight, to keep up with everything. When the kids became involved in activities, I did all I could do to be at every event, game, or performance to support them. I never had that kind of support as a child, and I know how much it hurt me. I did face some obstacles when it came to keeping my children actively involved. When they were in elementary school, activities like Girl Scouts and Boy Scouts, soccer, and dance were generally held in the evenings between five and seven. So picking them up from aftercare and getting them to those activities on time was a challenge. Scheduling activities around my jobs seemed impossible at times. However, making time for community and church activities like Bible study and choir for all of us was an intentional decision I refused to overlook. We did all of those things, year after year.

When I look back over our lives, I see that somehow God allowed me to be there for them despite all of their activities and my other obligations. I don't know how it all worked out, but somehow, He enabled the schedule to be under His authority so that I could love and support my children in everything. A schedule is something we choose to abide by. The Bible says, "We *plan* the way we want to live, but only God makes us able to live it" (Prov. 16:9 [MSG]). Another scripture says, "Put God in charge of your work, then what you've planned will take place" (Prov. 16:3 [MSG]).

I wanted them active during the summer. I felt keeping the kids focused in an activity was a godly principle and a way to align them with other principles that God teaches us. The Word says, "Through laziness, the rafters sag; because of idle hands, the house leaks" (Eccles. 10:18 [NIV]). I also believe keeping kids involved in activities provides an opportunity to encourage them in their faith. It also provides you with more opportunities to pray for their guidance and development.

As the kids got older and they became involved in even more activities and their own part-time jobs, it would have been very easy for us to fall into a routine where we barely spoke and just passed one another as we moved from room to room in the house. I know families who do that or whose members just sit in the same room and don't even speak to one another, supposedly because of tiredness. Despite us all having busy schedules, I refused to allow that kind of atmosphere in my home. God is a God of love and not division; He does not want us to exercise separation in our homes.

Work Is Good

My grandparents were strong advocates of work. They were in support of my first job at the age of thirteen. I worked as a shampoo girl at the local salon, washing hair for the stylists' clients. I loved it because I earned about thirteen dollars per week, and back then it was a huge paycheck! Likewise, in my home working was encouraged as soon as the kids were eligible to work. One of my daughter's focused activities for many years was dance and theater. She spent most of her summers training in ballet, jazz, and modern dance. In her performing arts studio, it was common for older kids to take on part-time jobs teaching dance classes to younger children. So my daughter's first work experience, at thirteen, was teaching a developmental tap class to children ages five to six. My son's first job, at the age of fourteen, was working at the local grocery store down the street. It was ideal because he could walk to work and during the summer, he could work a significant number of hours during the day.

The purpose of this wasn't to have them contribute to any bills or activities that were a part of my budget. In addition to keeping that focused level of activity high, it gave them the responsibility of working to earn money for extra things they wanted but that were not necessarily needed. We called it "chump change."

The term "chump change" was carried down from my grandparents' house to my own house. The term refers to how quickly a hard-earned paycheck can dwindle down to change. For example, a new video game, a new outfit, or going to a movie would be paid for with chump change. It helped them see how *spending* money often took place much faster than *earning* money. They learned to choose wisely what they spent their money on.

When they got to college, God allowed me to provide them with their own cars (another amazing miracle), but they were responsible for obtaining their own gas. They had to work and budget their money in order to afford gas.

I wanted them to understand how to build good financial security so they would not become comfortable with spending more than they could afford to and learn how not to live paycheck to paycheck. Working has taught them a few things based in biblical principle:

Proverbs 12:14

To value and appreciate hard work.

Matthew 25:21

To understand that good stewardship teaches us to manage small amounts so that we can be trusted with more.

Luke 6:38 and Malachi 3:10

To give offerings and to give a tenth of our earnings so it can be used in the body of Christ.

1 Corinthians 16:2

To know the importance of being debt-free and saving to meet our goals.

Ecclesiastes 3:1

To be patient and wise in our spending.

Both my children have worked consistently, from high school all the way through college and into their professional careers. They never refused to work or felt it was not their responsibility to work. By the time they graduated from college and took on full-time jobs, they both had almost a decade of work experience. They had a resume, references, and a developed, lifelong work ethic.

ENCOURAGEMENT

Building Them Up

In 1 Thessalonians 5, Paul reminds the people that we do not know the day nor the hour when Jesus will come, urging them in verse 11 to "encourage one another and build each other up." It is in God's plan that in the body of Christ we encourage one another until the day of our Savior's return.

It then becomes our responsibility to teach our children to be supportive and encouraging to others when they are young because the Bible tells us to do so. There are several places in the Old and New Testaments where the Word tells us to encourage one another, and we can certainly use these scriptures to support what we teach. But of course, a child will value their parent's consistent encouragement as the best example of how to encourage others and themselves.

Our children should feel us encouraging them in our conversations and actions. Even when we are disciplining them. Once the correction and, if necessary, punishment have been discussed, the child should still be encouraged to do better with the assurance that they can do so through Christ, who strengthens them.

Encouraging our kids in all areas of their lives is definitely something they will appreciate. Everyone wants to be acknowledged and built up by their brothers and sisters or mom and dad when they are sad, make a mistake, or are not confident in themselves about something. Building them up in the Word of God, with the knowledge that God always gets the glory, begins to build confidence that neither the parent nor the child may see. They will begin to feel good about themselves and others based on the Word of God, which builds leadership qualities within them.

Being built up in the Word enables our children to grow in their faith. If as the encourager the parent is using scripture (promises and principles) to encourage, when those things manifest, it allows the child to see God active in their life as a true and faithful God. Ultimately encouragement is just another form of love. That is why we see it so much in the Word of God, who is the God of love.

The Fear of Saying I Love You

I wanted my children to know without a doubt that they were loved by me. Part of the rejection I felt as a child was that I never really knew (or heard) that I was loved. The words "I love you" were never really said out loud in our family, except perhaps if someone was leaving for an extended period of time.

It seemed like there was an unspoken fear of the words or that saying I love you in basic conversation or discussions demonstrated some sort of weakness, especially among the men in our family. Even if the men in our family were told that someone loved them, they rarely returned the words.

I sort of assumed that somebody loved me. However, the guilt I felt about being raised by other people in the absence of my parents, combined with rarely ever hearing the words "I love you," really made me wonder if I was just an obligation to others.

The Bible is very clear that God wants us to know that He loves us. No doubting, questioning, wondering—it is clear that He loves us and He loves us despite what we have done or who we are.

I wanted my children to know they were loved, appreciated, valued, and unique. I wanted them to feel encouraged by the fact that despite their successes and failures, I still loved them. I wanted them to feel comfortable saying it to each other and to other people. I also wanted the words "I love you" to be commonly expressed in action and in words.

Silent Love Is Not Enough

Assuming your actions are enough is not enough. Providing food, clothes, a good home, and meeting a child's financial needs does not necessarily fully represent love for a child. While gifts and attending soccer games are demonstrations of love, children need more. Not only did I say I love you when we parted from one another, but I also said it during our daily check-ins, at the end of our family prayers, or simply when the Spirit of God led me to do so.

How often our children hear the words "I love you" should not be dependent on their age or sex. Teens and young adults need to hear it just as much as toddlers do. It's even more important as our children grow older because they are encountering more in life and in the world that will bring discouragement.

Our young boys and men should hear the words just as much as our daughters. Some people believe that telling a boy that they are loved too much will make them "weak." However, boys who know they are loved are more likely to become self-confident, strong men. If someone is taught to believe that fighting makes them strong, then that is what they will believe. On the other hand, if they are taught they are loved by their parents and God and this love is what makes them strong, they can be confident in this as well.

Acceptance versus Approval

In addition to speaking out about our love, we also have to make sure children are receiving our love and acceptance. There are lots of people, children and adults, who are loved but don't feel loved. We need to know that beyond hearing the words, our children really believe they are loved. A lack of confidence in this can essentially affect how someone feels about themselves, others, and the acceptance of Jesus in their lives.

It can also affect their choices, decisions, and relationships. But when we disagree on choices and decisions, it can make those in a relationship feel unloved. It is a great feeling to be around others who agree with your beliefs, opinions, and activities, which is why determining the difference between love and agreement and acceptance and approval can be so difficult.

The love we have for someone comes through accepting who they are, even if we do not always approve of what they do. God has instructed us to live our lives as Jesus did. When we study how Jesus treated others, we see He accepted all, although He did not always approve of their lifestyles. For example, Jesus accepted and defended an adulterous woman, but he did not approve of the relationship (John 8:2–11 [NIV]). Paul states in Romans 15:5–7 (NIV), "May the God who gives endurance and encouragement give you the same attitude of mind toward each other that Christ Jesus had, so that with one mind and one voice you may glorify the God and Father of our Lord Jesus Christ. Accept one another, then, just as Christ accepted you, in order to bring praise to God." In the scriptures we can see that God is a God of patience and encouragement and wants us to demonstrate that same attitude toward others. We also see that when we accept others the way Christ has accepted us, we are glorifying God.

Yet how do you, as a Christian parent, address the decisions that are not aligned theologically with the Word of God? Is the answer to reject the child and hope they will change?

Should you approve of the ungodly choice to demonstrate your acceptance of them? How do you encourage your child to move away from the decisions that God does not approve of and still share the love that Jesus did?

First, we remind our children that God loves us all regardless of our sin (Rom. 5:8 [NIV]). We do not ignore the child, or anyone else for that matter, as a way of demonstrating that our beliefs are important to us. In fact, such an action is hypocritical because it conflicts with the fact that God commands us to treat others with love, kindness, and patience. We should not ignore the behavior, nor should we constantly condemn or judge a child. What we pray for is the courage to speak out and discuss it with the child when God leads us and shows us how to respond. The parent should (1) be slow to speak and slow to anger (James 1:19 [NIV]); (2) keep the conversation gentle and not harsh (Prov. 15:1 [NIV]); (3) be positive rather than condescending (Col. 4:6 [NIV]); and (4) focus on the relevant issue and not on past mistakes (Isa. 43:18 [NIV]). Although this may be uncomfortable at times, it also creates an opportunity to encourage a child who may be struggling with shame and depression. You can pray with them and confirm that you love and accept them just as God does.

Destroying Generational Curses

Generational curses are sins repeated in a family over and over again, from generation to generation. Praying to break strongholds and generational curses in your children's lives is just as important as praying for God's grace and mercy. Sometimes we choose to ignore generational bondage or don't even recognize that we are operating within those patterns of sin. We don't recognize that our behaviors and tendencies can be observed by and developed in our children as they grow.

For example, years ago I recognized a pattern of unforgiveness, divorce, and hardened hearts, particularly with the women in my family, that manifested generation after generation. Of course, when I looked at my own life, I saw those very areas of bondage. When I began to study unforgiveness, I saw what a powerful stronghold it had on my life and how it was preventing my spiritual growth in so many ways. I had to learn to forgive others for the pain they had caused me, as well as forgive myself for what I viewed as failures in my life, including my divorce. But thank goodness the Bible says, "if anyone is in Christ, he is a new creation; old things have passed away: behold, all things have become new" (2 Cor. 5:17 [NKJV]).

Even if we don't recognize bondage or generational curses, we can ask God to reveal them to us through the Holy Spirit. We can then pray for our own deliverance and that our children be delivered as well. In Proverbs 13:22 (NKJV) the Word says that "a good man leaves an inheritance to his children's children," and so in my house, I always prayed for a good inheritance free of any generational curses, bondage, or strongholds.

Praying to break strongholds and generational curses in a child's life should definitely be a dedicated focused area of prayer for your children. Again, if you are not aware of what they are, simply pray. "Dear Lord, please free me, my family and my children of any curses or strongholds, seen or unseen, and break those chains of bondage in our lives this day and forevermore. Amen." Generational curses are real and a strategy of the enemy, but combatting them with prayer and God's Word is sufficient to rebuke and remove them from our lives.

Following Truth, Rejecting Lies

Although the Bible addresses everything we need, when we are struggling with a problem or new situation, trusting God in new things and for new promises can feel unfamiliar, and we may be less confident in our faith and declarations of those promises.

However, there are two very important scriptures in the Bible that can help us overcome all of those doubts and fears. These are two of my favorite scriptures as well. When I am wondering if I can trust God and His Word, I lean on these scriptures to get me through these times of waiting and trusting that His Word will be fulfilled. I view the scriptures to be faith-builders that remind us why we can trust God.

Numbers 23:19 (NLT) says, "God is not a man, so he does not lie. He is not human, so he does not change his mind. Has he ever spoken and failed to act? Has he ever promised and not carried it through?"

This scripture has been so encouraging to our family because we recognize God is perfect, an almighty God who is capable of all things. I know that I, as a human being, am not perfect and cannot provide all things as God can. There is a clear difference between us and God. Therefore, it is easier to accept that God in His supernatural, perfect Spirit is not capable of lying or making a promise that cannot be kept. At an early age, children should be taught what lying means. If a child understands that God cannot lie, it lays a firm foundation for the development of their faith and their relationship with God. It also motivates them not to lie in their own efforts to please Him.

The other key scripture tells us that God's Word will not return void. Isaiah 55:11 (AMP) says, "So will My word be which goes out of My mouth; It will not return to Me void (useless, without result), Without accomplishing what I desire, And without succeeding in the matter for which I sent it." This means the Word and plans of God will always be accomplished. Based on this scripture, I can be confident that if I am praying, trusting, and obeying the Word of God, it will be fulfilled in my life. The scripture also tells me that His Word has a purpose and that I can be confident this purpose will be achieved. These scriptures have brought an enormous amount of peace and joy to my life and to my family's lives.

When we know that God cannot lie and that His Word will always be fulfilled, we can reject the lies of the enemy. Two of Satan's most favored weapons for attacking our minds are doubt and fear. Satan wants us to believe that God will not do what God said He would do, especially when the promises of God do not come right away. Reminding children that Satan is the liar and that he only wants to "steal, kill and destroy" (John 10:10 [NIV]) strengthens their beliefs that we serve a God who is true and faithful.

However, reminding them that God does not lie is not the end of our responsibility. A child is not empowered to "know"

God's Word unless we teach it to them. We cannot ask them to replace a lie with truth if they don't know the truth. When the enemy attempted to invade my children's minds with a lie about something, I found the scripture that described what God said about the matter. Then we spoke together the written Word of God and then confessed Numbers 23:19 and Isaiah 55:11.

But let's step back a minute. How do we know what a child is thinking or whether they are being attacked with doubt and fear, especially when the child is older and thus less likely to share all their thoughts? I know that I encounter doubt and fear and am subject to the lies of the enemy. I think we all experience this. One way to encourage a child is to share situations in which you have had to overcome a lie by making the decision to follow the truth. You might disclose something from a past situation or even something you encountered that day. The point is guiding the child toward understanding we all fight battles to keep our minds in a place of truth.

Another way to help is to imagine how you would feel, from the position of a child, or even as an adult, if you were to encounter something that could invoke doubt or fear or wrong thinking. As I've mentioned, my children were involved in performing arts and sports and so they had to perform and play in front of people all the time. Maybe the fear of failure would cause them anxiety. Without any solicitation, I would say to them, "Remember, you can do all things through Christ who strengthens you" or remind them to call on the Lord because "the Lord will answer; you will cry for help, and he will say: Here am I" (Isa. 58:9 [NIV]).

For a child, sometimes there is peace in just knowing they can trust a parent to understand how they feel.

Overcoming Pain

Watching a child experience grief or pain can be extremely difficult. Regardless of the age of the child, a loving parent does not want to see their child in pain. God doesn't want to see us suffer either and wants us to lean on Him. He tells us what to do.

One example in scripture is 2 Corinthians 12:1–10 (MSG). Here Paul is speaking to the Corinthian church and describes his experience as a blind man and his encounter with Jesus.

> You've forced me to talk this way, and I do it
> against my better judgment. But now that we're
> at it, I may as well bring up the matter of vi-

sions and revelations that God gave me. For instance, I know a man who, fourteen years ago, was seized by Christ and swept in ecstasy to the heights of heaven. I really don't know if this took place in the body or out of it; only God knows. I also know that this man was hijacked into paradise—again, whether in or out of the body, I don't know; God knows. There he heard the unspeakable spoken, but was forbidden to tell what he heard. This is the man I want to talk about. But about myself, I'm not saying another word apart from the humiliations.

If I had a mind to brag a little, I could probably do it without looking ridiculous, and I'd still be speaking plain truth all the way. But I'll spare you. I don't want anyone imagining me as anything other than the fool you'd encounter if you saw me on the street or heard me talk.

Because of the extravagance of those revelations, and so I wouldn't get a big head, I was given the gift of a handicap to keep me in constant touch with my limitations. Satan's angel did his best to get me down; what he in fact did was push me to my knees. No danger then of walking around high and mighty! At first I didn't think of it as a gift, and begged God to remove it. Three times I did that, and then he told me,

My grace is enough; it's all you need.

My strength comes into its own in your weakness. Once I heard that, I was glad to let it happen. I quit focusing on the handicap and began appreciating the gift. It was a case of Christ's strength moving in on my weakness. Now I take limitations in stride, and with good cheer, these limitations that cut me down to size—abuse, accidents, opposition, bad breaks. I just let Christ take over! And so the weaker I get, the stronger I become.

He says to the people that if he "…had a mind to brag a little…" he could do it. Paul is referencing the fact that he could have mentioned his awesome experience in heaven and how he was given the ability to see visions and revelations. But he says he will spare the church those details and focus on the handicap that constantly reminds him of his limitations and weaknesses. After repeatedly calling out for God's help, God responds that His grace and power are enough for Paul's weaknesses.

I love the fact that Paul tells the church that after that experience, he began to view limitations differently. He says he views them with "good cheer," understanding he can let Christ "take over." He says, "The weaker I get, the stronger I become." We can learn to think the same way in times of weakness. We can assure our children that what Jesus did for Paul He will also do for us. When they are in pain, we can surround them with our love and share with them that Jesus's grace is sufficient for us. When it appears in the Bible, the word "grace" often means "favor" or "mercy." We can remind our children that our weaknesses are an opportunity for Christ's power to be made perfect in us. As we allow God to heal and deliver us, there is a testimony of His favor and strength to be seen in us.

Teaching children about God's grace and power in our times of weakness accomplishes a few things. As I stated before, it shows that God cares about our pain. When God heals us, it motivates our children to trust in God to a greater extent. When they encounter another disappointment, they learn to call out to Jesus with confidence that He will help them—just as He has helped them before.

Scriptures to share in times of pain:

2 Thessalonians 3:16

I will give you peace at all times and in every situation.

Proverbs 14:26

I will be your security and a safe place for your children.

Psalm 147:3

I will heal your broken heart and mend all your wounds.

1 Corinthians 10:13

I will not let you be tested beyond what you can endure.

Exodus 15:26

I am the Lord your God who heals all of your diseases.

Psalm 34:18

I am very close to those who have a broken heart.

Revelation 21:4

One day, I will wipe away every tear and take away all your pain.

Psalm 30:5

Your sadness may last for a night, but joy will come in the morning.

2 Chronicles 16:9

I look throughout the earth to strengthen those who belong to Me.

Nahum 1:7

The Lord is good, a refuge in times of trouble. He cares for those who trust in Him.

Opportunities to Encourage

Take advantage of every opportunity to encourage. Ask questions, watch for tone and body language changes, and remember effectively nosy moments provide great opportunities to encourage children. Even if you feel as though you've encouraged them in the same area repeatedly, do it again. If an accomplishment is repeated, or expanded, providing confirmation to a child that the parent is still proud and in support of their efforts is huge and goes a long way in motivating them to achieve more. It gives the parent an opportunity to give all the glory to God and encourage the child to do the same for their accomplishments.

When a child is upset or frustrated, prayer is important, but reminding the child that they can overcome the challenge because they are smart and strong can also provide so much comfort, reminding them that they do not have to be afraid. In 1 Timothy 1:7 (MSG), we read, "God doesn't want us to be shy with his gifts, but bold and loving and sensible." This is an opportunity to remind them they have God-given gifts. Point out examples of how you've seen those gifts used and how God has prepared us to use our gifts with success.

Recognizing gifts and identifying opportunities for encouragement should never end. A child is never too young or too old to receive encouragement. My children are young adults, but when they tell me about a wise decision they have made, I tell them it was a great choice and that they have really demonstrated good wisdom. When children become young adults and leave the house and are making life decisions on their own, it's especially important to continue to encourage them. Ask about their work life, social life, church, and friends so that you can encourage them in these areas and so there is no assumption on their part that you don't care because they are not there.

Encouraging a child is a huge opportunity for them to develop self-motivation. Often encouragement can be confused with motivation. Encouragement means providing support, hope, or confidence to someone, whereas motivation means someone has a reason to do something or is stimulated or enthusiastic in an interest or activity. I believe someone can be encouraged to find their motivation, but ultimately, motivation comes from within. For a parent, the key is knowing what is important to a child. It is easier for a child to develop motivation after receiving support and reassurance from people they know. For example, if a child has an interest in music, they may desire to improve their performance skills. They may motivate themselves to practice harder at it because of the support and confidence received from family and teachers. However, without encouragement a child may desire to improve, but lack motivation and choose to only practice with minimal time and effort because they view achieving higher goals as unattainable.

We should look at motivation as the process that initiates, guides, and maintains goal-oriented behaviors. Providing guidance when children encounter challenges or get off track can encourage them enough to remain motivated and engaged in their goals. They can be encouraged by their progress and how they have overcome their challenges. Encouraging a child to maintain their motivation to achieve their goals can also include reminding them of the benefits of accomplishing them.

Maintaining our motivation is definitely something we can all ask the Lord to help us with. We should ask that through the power of the Holy Spirit we receive strength to meet our aspirations and the wisdom in how to do it, even when it seems impossible. We are all able to encourage ourselves to meet our goals that align with the will of God if we consistently seek Him and confess the Word of God in our lives.

Identifying God-Given Gifts and Talents

All believers have at least one God-given gift and talent, and we should know what they are and use them. However, there are some distinct differences between gifts and talents. Both believers and nonbelievers have talents. A talent is exercised and developed and used for many different purposes. For example, if you have the natural ability to sing, it is pleasurable to hear you do so. You might sing to earn money or sing to entertain. As a believer, the talent of singing might also be used as a gift to evangelize and lead people to Christ through praise and worship.

A gift is given by the Holy Spirit only to Spirit-filled believers. According to 1 Corinthians 12:4–6 (NIV), "There are different kinds of gifts, but the same Spirit distributes them. There are different kinds of service, but the same Lord. There are different kinds of working, but in all of them and in everyone it is the same God at work." Paul teaches us about all of the spiritual gifts over the course of three different books of the Bible: Romans, Ephesians, and 1 Corinthians. They can be organized by studying the three main purposes of the gifts as they relate to the church and the body of Christ.

1. Apostles, prophets, evangelists, and pastor-teachers are seen as establishing gifts in the Bible. The gifts are intended to be used for planting seeds of faith, sharing the gospel, and the establishment of churches for growth (Eph. 4:11 and 1 Cor. 12:29).

2. Prophecy, service, teaching, encouragement, giving, administration/leadership, and mercy are supporting gifts, mostly used to organize and support churches so they may fulfill the responsibilities of the church (Rom. 12:6–8).

3. Wisdom, knowledge, faith, healing, miracles, prophecy, helps, administration, leadership, distinguishing spirits, speaking in

tongues, and interpreting tongues are gifts used by the Holy Spirit for the continual ministry of the church (1 Cor. 12:8–10, 27–31).

Notice there is overlap in the purposes of some of the gifts (i.e., leadership and administration) but the gift is used in the same way, generally speaking. Below are brief descriptions of the spiritual gifts:

APOSTLE: A person sent to new places with the gospel. An apostle can also provide leadership to other churches or ministries and offer advice on spiritual matters.

PROPHECY: The ability to speak the message of God to others. This sometimes involves foresight or visions of what is to come. This skill should be used only to offer encouragement or warning.

EVANGELISM: The ability to successfully communicate the message of the gospel, especially to nonbelievers.

TEACHING/PASTORING: The skill to teach from the Bible and communicate it effectively for the understanding and spiritual growth of others.

SERVING: Identifying and performing tasks needed for the body of Christ and using available resources to get the job done.

ENCOURAGEMENT/EXHORTATION: Competence in offering encouragement, comfort, and support to help someone be all that God wants them to be.

HELPS: Someone with this gift is able to support or assist members of the body of Christ so they may be free to minister to others.

HOSPITALITY: A natural ability to make people—even strangers—feel welcome in one's home or church as a means to disciple or serve them.

LEADERSHIP: This aptitude marks a person who is able to stand before a church, direct the body with care and attention, and motivate them toward achieving the church's goals.

ADMINISTRATION: The ability to help steer the church, or a ministry, toward the successful completion of God-given goals, with skills in planning, organization, and supervision.

MERCY: This is the defining trait of a person with great sensitivity for those who are suffering. It manifests itself in offering compassion and encouragement and in a love for giving practical help to someone in need.

WISDOM: The gift of being able to sort through facts and data to discover what needs to be done for a person, situation or the church.

KNOWLEDGE: This is the gift of someone who actively pursues knowledge of the Bible. This person may also enjoy analyzing biblical data.

FAITH: People with this gift have such great confidence in the power and promises of God that they can stand strong in their belief no matter what may try to shake them. They can also stand up for the church and for their faith in such a way as to defend and move it forward.

HEALING: A capability used by God to restore others, be it physically, emotionally, mentally, or spiritually.

DISCERNMENT: The wisdom to distinguish truth from untruth by correctly evaluating whether a behavior or teaching is from God or another, ungodly source.

GIVING: Those who have this gift are particularly willing and able to share what resources they have with pleasure and without the need to see them returned.

SPEAKING IN TONGUES: The supernatural ability to speak in another language (one that has not been learned).

INTERPRETING TONGUES: The ability to interpret, understand, and provide the meaning of tongues.

Since the goal is for our children to give their life to Christ at an early age, we also want to encourage them to seek out their gifts and use them whenever God desires. A child may ask you to help them determine what their gifts and talents are. One suggestion would be to ask what they like to do or believe they are good at and then ask whether they believe it could be used to help others in the body of Christ.

If you are unsure what their gifts are, pray and ask God to show you. Once you've prayed and come to understand what the gifts of the Spirit are, be watchful of the opportunities that are presented for those gifts to be used. Sometimes God confirms things to us by providing opportunities to apply what He has told us in our day-to-day lives.

We want our children to practice walking in their gifts so they feel confident to use them. The Bible says that we are to use gifts in accordance with our faith (Rom. 12:6 [NIV]), so if we encourage our children to walk in faith as they use God's gifts, their relationship with God grows and their spiritual maturity grows. Explain that when we all use the spiritual gifts God has given us, the body of Christ works better. Point out examples of spiritual gifts used by others and by your children themselves. I can remember telling my children all the time how I recognized some of the spiritual gifts I saw in them. Today I can clearly see the gifts of apostleship, prophecy, evangelism, teaching, serving, faith, healing, wisdom, knowledge, and discernment continue to develop and manifest in their lives.

Maintaining Good Family Relationships

It would be great if we could say that every family member has a wonderful relationship with every other family member in their family. I can definitely say that's not the case in mine. But even when such a situation isn't in place, we should all be striving toward developing and maintaining strong relationships, especially with our immediate family members. Aside from our relationship with God, our relationships with our mothers, fathers, and siblings are the most significant to us. We should be able to encourage and rely on these people with the confidence of knowing we can trust them, that they can trust us, and that we will always have one another's backs.

Establishing that type of relationship is built on the fruits of the spirit, and more specifically love, as described in 1 Corinthians 13:4–8 (NIV). The scripture states that love "always protects, always trusts, always hopes, always perseveres" (1 Cor. 13:7 [NIV]). Once again, maintaining that kind of relationship is based on forgiveness. Forgiveness allows us to recognize that we are not perfect. Jesus says, "Be merciful, just as your Father is merciful. Do not judge, and you will not be judged. Do not condemn, and you will not be condemned. Forgive, and you will be forgiven" (Luke 6:36–37 [NIV]).

Choosing to ignore unforgiveness, bitterness, and division in the home provides the enemy the pathway to tear down relationships. Rather than allowing that, a parent must be aware of it and address it with communication that encourages everyone to participate with a loving and forgiving heart. It is not acceptable to let people storm off in anger to other rooms and not discuss the problem. When hurtful things are said, they should be addressed and not ignored. We should be mindful of what we say to others, acknowledging that words can hurt. Fighting the enemy to maintain strong relationships is an ongoing war but a necessary one. God tells us, "Remember the Lord, who is great and awesome, and fight for your families, your sons and your daughters, your wives and your homes" (Neh. 4:14 [NIV]). We need strong Christian relationships within our families because the world we live in is full of evil division.

Encouraging family members to take an interest in the lives of each other is important to building great family relationships as well. This makes the family members feel supported by their loved ones. Parents who encourage their children to support their siblings can foster genuine friendships between siblings and a desire in them to independently support one another throughout their lives. My children have always had that kind of relationship. I remember when my son was sick, my daughter posted a request on her social media page for everyone to "please pray for my favorite person on the earth." It warms my heart to know the degree of love and support they have for one another.

Encourage the Encourager

Teaching children to encourage others is an important part of Christian parenting. It would actually be rather selfish for them and us to always be on the receiving end of encouragement. God's Word teaches us to give and receive. Teaching our children to be the encourager enables them to be in a position to give to others rather than always focusing on themselves.

If encouraging others does not seem to be a natural gift for your child, point out opportunities for them to offer encouragement to others. Point out situations with family members and friends where they can build them up with the Word of God. Encourage them to do this in their ministry and volunteer work, activities, and community service. If they are shy about reaching out to someone, remind them how they feel when they are looking for support and love from others. Remind them what it feels like when someone offers them a little bit of support that provides hope and peace. Perhaps the same promise of God that you've given to them that day they can offer to someone else. Helping someone doesn't always have to come with words. Listening when someone needs to talk, spending time with them, or helping them do something are also ways to offer support. These actions or gifts can be equally encouraging.

In Romans 14:19–20 (MSG), Paul tells us to "use all our energy in getting along with each other. Help others with encouraging words." In Hebrews 3:13 (AMP), the scripture says to "encourage one another every day, as long as it is called 'Today,' so that none of you will be hardened by the deceitfulness of sin." So not only should we use "all our energy" to encourage others, but we should also do it daily. As often as we see in the bible the instruction to encourage others, I would venture to say that teaching this to our children is important in the eyes of God.

We can ask Him to show us ways to encourage someone each day, as the Word tells us to do. Praying to God with our children for Him to make us better at encouraging others is something we can definitely do.

A PRAYER TO SHARE

Raising children who love God is a God-given purpose He has provided us as parents. He loves us and our children unconditionally. Through our prayers and trust in God, we can raise wonderful Spirit-filled children who seek Him with a true desire to serve Him. We are blessed to teach our children what an honor it is to serve God the Father, God the Son, and God the Spirit with reverence, praise, and worship. As we accept our responsibility—and privilege—to teach our children who God is and how He wants to bless us, we are preparing them for an abundant life to live here on earth, as well as eternally in heaven!

This is a prayer I share with every parent:

Dear Heavenly Father,

Our almighty and faithful Father, let every parent who desires to seek your wisdom and discernment receive your guidance. As we recognize that our children are holy gifts from you, Father, teach us how to raise them in a manner that is pleasing to you. Show us through the power of the Holy Spirit how to pray on their behalf. Show us how to train them so that when they grow old, they will not depart from you or your Word. Help them to establish a firm foundation in you with your Word planted in their hearts. Allow them to walk by faith with testimonies of their own to share with others. Use them as your vessels to establish the work of your kingdom here on earth and in heaven. I pray for healthy, godly relationships throughout their lives. I ask that you deliver them from any sin or temptations they fall to and allow them to overcome any guilt or shame. Always remind them that they are redeemed by the blood of

Christ, who has paid the price for their sins. I pray for deliverance and protection against disease, pain, bondage, and suffering and instead declare healing, peace, and provision in their lives. Let your love surround them and encourage them in what you have called them to do. Teach them to love others as you have loved us. I pray they will worship and obey you all the days of their lives. Thank you, Lord. It is in Jesus's name I pray.

Amen.